Managing
People

BEST PRACTICES:
Managing
People

SECRETS TO LEADING FOR NEW MANAGERS

BARRY SILVERSTEIN

An Imprint of HarperCollins*Publishers*

HarperCollins books may be purchased for educational,
business, or sales promotional use. For information,
please write: Special Markets Department, HarperCollins
Publishers, 10 East 53rd Street, New York, NY 10022.

Produced for HarperCollins by:

HYDRA PUBLISHING
129 MAIN STREET
IRVINGTON, NY 10533
WWW.HYLASPUBLISHING.COM

FIRST EDITION

ISBN: 978-0-06-114556-8

07 08 09 10 11   RRD   10 9 8 7 6 5 4 3 2

Barry Silverstein is a business writer and management consultant. He has 30 years of experience managing and motivating people in small and large businesses. He founded his own direct and Internet marketing agency and ran it for 20 years, growing it to a $5 million, 50-person organization. He also held management positions with Xerox Corporation and advertising agency Arnold Worldwide.

Silverstein is the author of three titles in the Collins Best Practices series. He is also the coauthor of *The Breakaway Brand* (McGraw-Hill, 2005) and the author of *Business-to-Business Internet Marketing* (Maximum Press, 2001) and *Internet Marketing for Information Technology Companies* (Maximum Press, 2001).

Contents

Preface

How do you hire people? How do you encourage them to do a better job? What do you say to them if they don't? How do you fire someone who refuses to cooperate? How do you get your staff on board at a time of major change?

In this book, we distill the wisdom of some of the best minds in the field to tell you how to do a better job at managing your employees and creating a workplace that supports the goals of your company. The language is simple and the design colorful to make the information easy to grasp.

Quizzes help you assess your knowledge of people and project management issues. Case files show how companies have tackled tough management problems. Sidebars give you a big-picture look at management challenges and highlight innovative, out-of-the-box solutions worth considering. Quotes from business leaders will inspire you as you face your own challenges. Finally, in case you want to dig deeper into management issues, we recommend some of the most important business books available. The authors of these books both influence and reflect today's thinking about managing people and related issues. Understanding the ideas they cover will inspire you as a manager.

Even if you don't dip into these volumes, the knowledge you gain from studying the pages of this book will equip you to deal firmly, effectively, and insightfully with the management issues you face every day—to help you make a difference to your company and in the lives of the people who support you.

THE EDITORS

Managing People 101

"The task of management is to make people capable of joint performance, to make their strengths effective and their weaknesses irrelevant."

—Peter Drucker,
management guru and author
(1909–2005)

Managing people isn't like managing things or even like managing projects. Each person has unique capabilities and talents, strengths and weaknesses—and feelings. Helping each person achieve his or her individual potential may require different motivational strategies and tactics.

Self-Assessment Quiz

ARE YOU MANAGEMENT MATERIAL?

Read each of the following statements and indicate whether you agree or disagree. Then check your score at the end.

1. I consider myself a good judge of character.
   - ◯ Agree   ◯ Disagree

2. I trust people to do the right thing.
   - ◯ Agree   ◯ Disagree

3. If someone comes to me with a problem at work, I take time to listen and offer help without being judgmental.
   - ◯ Agree   ◯ Disagree

4. When a co-worker doesn't understand something, I don't lose my patience.
   - ◯ Agree   ◯ Disagree

5. I think it is best not to be very close friends with someone I manage.
   - ◯ Agree   ◯ Disagree

6. It is better to make the right decision than a popular one.
   - ◯ Agree   ◯ Disagree

7. I'm good at delegating work.
   ○ Agree   ○ Disagree

8. I know how to motivate people.
   ○ Agree   ○ Disagree

9. It is better to give instructions than orders.
   ○ Agree   ○ Disagree

10. People would say I have integrity.
    ○ Agree   ○ Disagree

Scoring

Give yourself 1 point for every question you answered "Agree" and 0 points for every question you answered "Disagree."

Analysis

8–10   You have the potential to be an excellent manager of people.

5–7   You could use some work on people-management skills.

0–4   You have a lot more to learn if you want to effectively manage people.

What It Takes to Be a Good Manager

Before you can effectively manage other people, you need to know about yourself and your management abilities. The Self-Assessment Quiz on pages 2–3 will help you understand what skills you bring to the game.

"If your staff is happy, you are doing your job. People don't often leave jobs—and, in particular, bosses—they like. Treat people the right way and you will have disciples for life."

—Tom Markert,
author of *You Can't Win a Fight with Your Boss*

Managing people used to mean dominating them. The boss's word was absolute and not to be questioned. But today's workplace is very different. As companies continue to increase productivity and reduce costs, operations tend to be consolidated: a smaller number of people do a greater amount of work with fewer managers.

To succeed in this climate, businesses depend on knowledge-sharing, effective communication, and teamwork. These are difficult to achieve without the three C's described on pages 6–7.

The BIG Picture

THE MANAGER'S PERSPECTIVE

The manager's perspective needs to be broad and all-encompassing. As a manager, you are the one who needs to understand what must get done, what it will take to accomplish your goal, how to assess and monitor progress, and how to measure success at the completion of the work.

Take advantage of the capabilities of each of your staff members and delegate the appropriate tasks so they can work as a team towards a common goal. Match specific tasks to the skills of each individual. Help and guide them—but let them do the work. Hold team progress meetings to keep everyone on track and follow up individually with any team member who is having trouble or falling behind.

Like a great maestro conducting an orchestra, you are there to keep every individual working in harmony and to ensure that the end result is a beautifully executed performance.

Behind the Numbers

DECLINE IN MIDDLE MANAGERS

During the 13 years between 1986 and 1999, the number of middle managers in large corporations declined by 27 percent. This study reflects the reality of more than 300 publicly traded U.S. firms.

▪ Firm size = Number of employees in thousands

▪ Depth = Number of managers between CEO and Divisional Manager

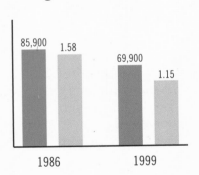

SOURCE: "The Flattening Firm" by Raghuram Rajan and Julie Wulf, National Bureau of Economic Research (April 2003).

Collaboration. A good manager creates many opportunities for people to collaborate in setting goals, determining how work will get accomplished, and establishing criteria to measure a project's success rate.

Cooperation. Fostering cooperation within a work group and setting a good example as a manager encourages employees to focus on the needs of the group rather than only on their own needs.

Consensus. Establishing consensus among your workers creates a common sense of purpose and involves everyone in working toward the same goal. Good managers use consensus-building to encourage employees to voice opinions while maintaining control of the group.

What's Your Management Style?

Managers can have very different styles and still succeed.

At one extreme are autocratic, heavy-handed managers who govern by fear and intimidation.

• POWER POINTS •

SECRETS OF MANAGERIAL SUCCESS

Effective people managers practice the fine art of delegation.

- They delegate tasks without abdicating their responsibility.

- They explain the *why* but never dictate the *how*.

- They give instructions, not orders.

Dos & Don'ts ☑

MANAGEMENT RULES TO LIVE BY

As a manager, you need to hold yourself to a high standard.

☐ Do lead by example.

☐ Don't manage by fear and intimidation.

☐ Do plan your work and work your plan.

☐ Don't begin a plan without a specific goal.

☐ Don't fail to plan for things going wrong.

☐ Don't let your team begin a project without a common goal.

☐ Do keep a positive attitude.

☐ Do give instructions, not orders.

☐ Don't overdelegate.

☐ Don't abdicate your responsibility for the outcome of a goal.

☐ Do foster collaboration and teamwork.

In the long term, this generates ill will and lack of respect; employees either contribute minimally or eventually choose to work elsewhere.

At the other extreme are managers with a nice-guy approach. They fraternize with employees, delegate almost everything, and generally take a

- ☐ Do catch people doing something right.
- ☐ Do create opportunities for people to succeed.
- ☐ Do empower subordinates with responsibility.
- ☐ Don't criticize your staff in public.
- ☐ Do fix the problem, not the blame.
- ☐ Don't be dishonest when you have bad news to deliver.
- ☐ Don't tune out an employee who is telling you something you don't want to hear.
- ☐ Do listen before you speak.
- ☐ Do encourage an open, honest work environment.

hands-off attitude. This management style can be almost as detrimental as the autocratic style; the overall lack of direction can frustrate employees.

For the most part, good managers of people exhibit some of both styles when appropriate, and with balance. Good managers combine solid direction and strong leadership with objectivity, compassion, and the right amount of delegation. Whatever your style, it is important to be consistent and fair.

It also pays to get to know the people who work for you. Ask them questions and solicit their input and advice. Then listen to what they have to say. Just taking the time to listen to your staff—to hear and respect their opinions and to "agree to disagree" if necessary—makes a big difference.

Managers Versus Leaders

Managers tend to be more rational, objective, and driven by organizational needs, while leaders are more visionary, emotional, and inspirational in nature.

Although the ideal for a good manager is to be a good leader as well, it doesn't always work out that way. A great leader has drive and personality in addition to management ability. A great manager may lack those qualities. However, some managers can also become great leaders. While becoming a leader is something to strive for, the transformation is never a sure thing.

The Fine Art of Delegation

One of the most important skills a good manager must acquire is how to delegate.

There is a difference between *delegation* and *abdication*. You can't just drop a project on someone's desk and hope he or she will figure it out—that would be abdicating your responsibility as a manager. Instead, a good manager first gives thought to which tasks are appropriate to delegate to which employees and then diligently follows up to be sure each task has been successfully completed.

An effective manager explains the *why* of the task and establishes goals, due dates, and criteria to measure success. But a manager should not detail the *how*. It is the employee's responsibility to take ownership of the job and determine the best way to get it done.

> "Good management consists in showing average people how to do the work of superior people."
>
> —John D. Rockefeller,
> American industrialist and
> founder of Standard Oil
> (1839–1937)

When you delegate, give *instructions* rather than *orders*. Instructions acknowledge that the individual receiving them is capable of participating, learning, and doing. Instructions invite people to have a say in how things are done. Orders imply that there is one right way to do something, which discourages employees from thinking independently or showing initiative.

It takes a large measure of trust to delegate. You must recognize that the employee's path to the outcome may not be exactly the one you would have taken.

Overburdening an employee with work is as bad as overmonitoring work that you have delegated. Delegate the right work to the right

> "Don't tell people how to do things. Tell them what to do and let them surprise you with their results."
>
> —George S. Patton,
> U.S. general
> (1885–1945)

people, give them enough leeway to accomplish what needs to be done, and monitor their progress reasonably and effectively so that they feel supported rather than micromanaged.

Praise in Public, Criticize in Private

As a manager, you are likely to have your share of positive and negative experiences with employees.

Be sure to praise an employee publicly when you catch him or her doing something right. Praise the individual for the specific action and be honest and sincere about it.

CASE *FILE*

TURNAROUND SPECIALIST

New senior managers brought in to rescue a corporation in trouble are often faced with challenging decisions.

Such was the case of Lou Gerstner, credited with rejuvenating IBM during his tenure as CEO from 1993 to 2002.

When he came to IBM, Gerstner discovered a company in which managers of operating units competed with one another. Employees focused on their own internal issues rather than those of their customers.

Gerstner made an effort to get everyone working towards a common purpose. Specifically, he instituted rewards based on total corporate performance instead of division or unit performance.

As Gerstner wrote, "During my time at IBM, I came to see that culture isn't just one aspect of the game—it is the game. In the end, an organization is nothing more than the collective capacity of its people to create value."

SOURCE: *Who Says Elephants Can't Dance* by Louis V. Gerstner, Jr. (Collins, 2002).

Dos & Don'ts ☑

DEAL WITH IT

A strong manager is always looking down the road. When a job is well done, it deserves praise. When an employee does something wrong, criticism may be appropriate. But remember to use a light touch.

☐ Do get to know your staff.

☐ Do start planning your course of action as soon as you see clouds on the horizon.

☐ Don't wait to address a problem.

☐ Do get to the root of the problem.

☐ Do encourage the individual to talk openly without fear of reprimand.

If an employee requires criticism, however, keep it private. Deliver negative feedback as soon as you can after a poor performance or an instance of unacceptable behavior. Speak with the employee calmly, without becoming emotional or heated. Always criticize the employee's specific behavior or performance, not the person's character. Give the employee the opportunity to explain why the behavior or incident occurred.

Finally, help the employee create and implement a positive plan to prevent it from

- [ ] Do work out a solution. Come to a resolution that respects the person while maintaining your authority.

- [ ] Don't berate an employee in front of others.

- [ ] Don't criticize the individual. Focus instead on the individual's actions or performance.

- [ ] Don't get emotional when criticizing.

- [ ] Don't be sweepingly negative. Point to specific actions or incidents instead—and do it soon after they have occurred.

- [ ] Don't stifle a chance for dialogue.

happening again. Agree on a goal and a timeline. And then move on.

Turn Problems into Opportunities

Managing people isn't always predictable. Some people come to a job with personal baggage that can cause them to become emotional, to over-react, or to object to authority.

As a manager, you need to get to know the people who work for you as individuals. Meet with all your staff members individually, one at a time. Find out more about what they do every day, what decisions they make, and what challenges them.

What complaints do they get on a regular basis? What misunderstandings have arisen? What makes them angry? What was efficient and what took too long? Which procedures are too complicated?

Ask about their goals, determine their likes and dislikes, and assess their personality styles.

CASE *FILE*

MANAGING A CINDERELLA STORY

During the 2006 NCAA Men's Basketball Tournament, one of the most improbable things happened in the history of the tournament: Little-known George Mason University reached the Final Four.

Coach Jim Larranaga was largely credited for the team's success. He was human and approachable, often inviting team members to his home. Yet at the same time he held his players to a high standard of excellence. During a conference semifinal game, Larranaga saw one of his best players commit a serious foul that the officials missed. The coach himself benched the player.

Then, for each person, ask yourself:
- How does this person's job fit with the others?
- In what ways can I best use this person's knowledge, experience, and skill set?
- Is this person a leader or a follower?
- Will this person present a management challenge in any way?

Good managers draw on their knowledge of their staffs' strengths, weaknesses, and preferences when orchestrating company work.

"Outstanding leaders go out of their way to boost the self-esteem of their personnel. If people believe in themselves, it's amazing what they can accomplish."

—Sam Walton,
founder of Wal-Mart

Sometimes management challenges turn out to be opportunities. The flip side of a maddeningly difficult quality can be a strength on a specific project. For instance, an individual who demonstrates a lack of flexibility may be just the hyperorganized, methodical, and detail-oriented person you need for your next big project.

Plan Your Work and Work Your Plan

A manager can accomplish very little without a plan of action. Start by establishing a goal. Then figure out what it will take to reach that goal. What staff will you need? What resources will be required? Are there budget constraints? What efficiencies can you achieve? What contingencies will you have if things go wrong?

Next, work your plan. Create a step-by-step plan of action for accomplishing your goal. Assemble everything you need and get started.

Provide a common purpose and good direction to your staff and delegate appropriately along the way.

• POWER POINTS •

WHAT TO INCLUDE IN YOUR PLANS

Good managers plan their work carefully. Here are the elements of a plan:

- Setting goals

- Orchestrating staff buy-in

- Defining resources—staff, outside suppliers, budget

- Determining each step

- Identifying achievable milestones

- Anticipating snafus and setting up a plan B for each one

"Excellent companies
are the way they are
because they are
organized to obtain
extraordinary effort from
ordinary human beings."

—Tom Peters and Robert H. Waterman, Jr.,
authors of *In Search of Excellence*

The key word here is *delegate*. This does not
mean stepping aside entirely. Be supportive,
involved, and available. Help your people succeed. Monitor progress from beginning to end,
and step in as necessary to provide direction or
keep things on track. Strive for success. At the
same time, look ahead, anticipating what could
go wrong. Have contingencies and alternative
plans available just in case things don't turn out
as anticipated.

Finally, when your goal is reached, always let
your staff know how much you appreciate their
hard work.

Essential Skill I
Managing Individuals

"A great manager is brilliant at spotting the unique differences that separate each person and then capitalizing on them."

—Marcus Buckingham, coauthor of *Now, Discover Your Strengths*

Regardless of your organization's size, as a manager you are faced with the same basic challenge: You manage individuals, not just teams, work groups, departments, or divisions. Consequently, you need to understand each individual's strengths, weaknesses, talents, abilities, and goals.

You must be aware of any organizational, emotional, or work-environment issues that could be affecting an individual's job performance. You have to be patient and calm, and at the same time find ways to keep people motivated so that work is accomplished and progress is made.

While no two people are alike, there are certain sound management principles you can always apply to make your job easier.

First: Remember that you have a significant impact on an individual's job satisfaction and career development. This is a serious responsibility, one that provides you with the opportunity to participate in someone's success. Nurturing employees, guiding them along the way, and watching them achieve their goals can be one of the most rewarding things about management.

• POWER POINTS •

ELEMENTS OF SUCCESS

Whether employees do well at work has everything to do with the competence and conscientiousness of their managers. To succeed they need the following:

- Effective training

- Honest, regular feedback—both positive and negative

- Access to the information and tools they need to make good decisions

Second: Recruit and hire the right people, then give them the training and tools they need to do their jobs well. When you bring quality people into your organization, or promote outstanding workers from within, you are establishing a standard of excellence.

Third: Help individuals monitor their progress by providing objective, constructive, and timely feedback, both informally and during performance reviews. Take the attitude that you expect your staff to succeed. Help them see the benefits associated with doing their jobs well and they

COMBAT WANING ENTHUSIASM

To manage individuals most effectively, it is important to get off to a good start. Surveys of some 1.2 million employees at 52 primarily large companies found that a majority of employees are enthusiastic when they start a new job. But their morale declines sharply after six months and continues to do so for the next several years. Managers who foster good relationships with new employees have a much better chance of keeping them motivated.

SOURCE: "Stop Demotivating Your Employees!" by David Sirota et al., *Harvard Management Update* (January 2006).

THE BOTTOM LINE

Dos & Don'ts ☑

PUTTING PEOPLE FIRST

Great managers learn how to get the most out of their staff.

☐ Do believe in a person's ability to succeed and do the right thing.

☐ Do listen responsively.

☐ Do get out of your office—let your staff see that you care about them.

☐ Don't wait to act on a problem someone brings to you.

☐ Do ask how each person is doing.

☐ Don't let people struggle—find out what you can do to help them do their jobs more effectively.

will be more satisfied. You will gain more satisfaction from your job as well.

Fourth: Manage with compassion and honesty, instead of by fear or by creating uncertainty. Managers who are approachable, personable, and forthright have greater success than those who tend to be remote, tight with information, or unavailable. Adopt a more accessible management style and you will have employees who are happier and more likely to stay in their jobs.

Finally: Communicate the big picture, create a game plan, and set a positive tone for achieving a goal. If you can effectively present your vision to your staff and inspire them, they will want to join you in contributing to the team's success.

SELECTING STAFF

How do you hire the right person for the job? You can remove some of the guesswork by creating a clear job description and instituting an orderly screening, interview, and decision process.

The Job Description

First, you must identify exactly what you need and define your requirements. Create a detailed

Red Flags ✖◆

ARE YOU BEING COUNTERPRODUCTIVE?

Check yourself for these behaviors, which could make you counterproductive as a manager:

- **The cutoff** – You impatiently interrupt people.

- **The false positive** – You sugar-coat bad news instead of delivering it directly and honestly.

- **The shifty-eyed shuffle** – You avoid making eye contact, or seem tense while speaking to an employee.

- **The dump and run** – You tend to delegate a lot of work with little or no explanation.

job description that includes the job title, objective, specific responsibilities, and how the job fits into the organization's reporting structure.

Be as specific as possible in describing the qualifications and requirements for the job: number of years of experience, needed skills, education, particular traits (such as meticulousness or organizational skills), and special proficiencies (familiarity with a computer program, knowledge of a foreign language). Establish a salary range for the position.

• POWER POINTS •

JOB DESCRIPTION BASICS

Choosing the best possible candidate begins with a strong job description that includes all the essentials about the job:

- Title
- Job objective
- Duties and responsibilities
- Reporting structure
- Salary
- Experience and education required
- Skills and proficiencies needed
- Applicable qualities of mind
- Intangibles

While deciding what your actual requirements are and what the job description should include, also give careful thought to intangibles. Think about your own management style and your company's culture. Ask yourself what type of person would be the best match. Make a list of all the characteristics your ideal candidate for the position would have.

> "You will be great exactly to the extent that you are willing and eager to hire people who are better than you."
>
> —Tom Peters

Former General Electric CEO Jack Welch emphasizes the importance of three qualities above all others in employees: integrity, intelligence, and maturity. In considering candidates for the job, pay attention to these valuable underlying characteristics. They will stand you in good stead as you meet the challenges of the workplace together.

The Screening Process

In larger organizations, candidates' applications and resumes might initially be screened

> "Every staffing need must begin with a clear assessment of the work: Exactly which tasks, responsibilities, and projects need to be done? Once you have a clear picture of the work itself, the remaining questions are obvious: Who is the best person for this job? Where will you find the people you need?"
>
> —Bruce Tulgan,
> author of *Winning the Talent Wars*

by recruiters working either for your company's human resources (HR) department or for an outside firm. It's often a good idea to keep this screening fairly loose the first time around so that you can review as many candidates as possible. If appropriate, consider internal candidates for the position. Review their qualifications objectively.

Applications and resumes are your best guide to experience and qualifications. As an indicator of how well a candidate communicates, the cover letter accompanying a resume is equally important. It can also give you an idea of the individual's personality, style, motivation, and attention to detail.

Use a consistent method for ranking the candidates. One common approach is to sort prospects' applications into three separate groups: one for strong candidates, one for likely

Plan B

THE BAD HIRE

You did all the right things and selected the best candidate. But after the person has been in the job for a few months, you have the awful realization that he or she is a bad fit.

If others agree with your assessment, you've given the person every chance to improve, and you feel there is no way you can salvage the situation, it's best to let the individual go rather than prolong the problem.

Be specific when you explain why it isn't working out and be generous with severance.

Then cut your losses and move on.

Dos & Don'ts ☑

INTERVIEW QUESTIONS

Know what you want to ask—and know which topics are off limits.

☐ Don't ask about the candidate's age, race, or ethnicity.

☐ Don't ask about marital or family status.

☐ Don't ask about living or child-care arrangements.

☐ Don't ask about physical or mental disabilities.

☐ Don't ask about someone's credit history or financial situation.

☐ Do ask how prior positions have prepared her for this job.

candidates, and one for candidates who are obviously not qualified.

The strong resumes can then be arranged in order of your interest in the candidates, or divided into several subgroups based on your assessment of the candidates' particular strengths.

The Interview

Interview your strongest candidates personally. Have a few other people interview the strong

☐ Do explore what she hopes to bring to the company.

☐ Do find out what his experience has taught him about working with other people.

☐ Do probe his reasons for leaving his current position.

☐ Do ask how she dealt with a challenge at a previous position and what she learned.

☐ Do ask about problems she had with co-workers in the past and how they were resolved.

☐ Do ask if the candidate has questions for you.

candidates as well. For the candidates, it is usually less intimidating to meet with interviewers individually. At least one of the interviewers should be in the same work group or hold a position similar to the job for which you are hiring.

Asking the right questions during an interview will give you the input you need to make an informed decision. Does the candidate seem genuine? Does she admit to mistakes? How does he discuss his life—is he candid yet appropriately discreet? Is she intellectually curious? Does she seem knowledgeable not only about her field but also about a range of topics? Finally, does your gut tell you he will be able to handle stress? Does he respect others? Does she have a sense of humor?

> ## "Every minute devoted to putting the proper person in the proper slot is worth weeks of time later."
>
> —Colman Mockler,
> former CEO of Gillette
> (1930–1991)

It's a good plan to have everyone who interviews a candidate ask the same basic questions about prior experience, job qualifications, and management ability so you can directly compare the answers.

Make sure you know which questions are off limits for legal reasons. If a question does not relate directly to the individual's performance, do not ask it.

Finally, find out if the candidate has questions for you. Smart questions from a candidate are as important a consideration as good answers to your questions.

Watch the candidate carefully as he or she speaks. Observe body language and evaluate the individual's ability to think.

After the interview, write down your impressions right away. Make sure to include your gut reaction—your feeling about your chemistry or rapport with the candidate—as well as your impression of the individual's experience and qualifications. Do you think this person would fit in? Would he or she work well with you, your group, and your company?

• POWER POINTS •

INTERVIEWING THAT WORKS

When interviewing candidates, an orderly process is most effective:

- Rank candidates.

- Decide who will do interviews.

- Prepare a list of initial questions and possible follow-ups.

- Cover all relevant topics during the interview.

- Reflect on your interview and gut reactions to the candidate.

- Compare candidates' answers with your interview team.

First impressions may be lasting, but it's a good idea to regroup with the other interviewers and consider their thoughts about each candidate. Bring finalists back for second interviews to ask additional questions, or to explore experiences and qualifications that seem especially pertinent to the job.

The Final Decision

A number of factors enter into a final hiring decision—the candidate's experience, qualifications, references, and salary requirements as well as your and your fellow interviewers' impressions about the candidate's suitability for the position and fit with your team.

It's important to have a solid sense that you have found the right person for the position before you make a job offer. You and your company will be making a significant investment in this individual. You want it to pay off.

TRAINING

An old adage in business: There is never enough time to do it right—but there's always time to do it over. One of the most common reasons that tasks are mishandled the first time around is the employee's lack of proper training.

Managers who appreciate the importance of training display a love of learning and function as role models for their staff. Periodically, they take courses to improve their own skills, and they encourage their employees to do the same. Managers who train and coach others derive satisfaction from teaching and mentoring while

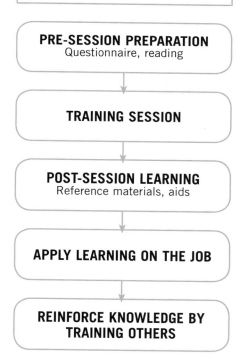

WORK**FLOW** TOOLS

EMPLOYEE TRAINING CYCLE

PRE-SESSION PREPARATION
Questionnaire, reading

↓

TRAINING SESSION

↓

POST-SESSION LEARNING
Reference materials, aids

↓

APPLY LEARNING ON THE JOB

↓

REINFORCE KNOWLEDGE BY TRAINING OTHERS

at the same time improving their own communication skills. Staff training takes place in various ways—in new-employee orientation sessions, in formal training courses, and via on-the-job training, as appropriate.

A formal assessment can help determine the type of training that would be most useful for your staff. Typically conducted by human

• POWER POINTS •

KEEP EMPLOYEES LEARNING

Giving your staff the knowledge they need to do a better job pays off. You can provide this enrichment in several ways:

- Formal introductory and refresher courses
- Remedial courses for employees lacking a specific skill
- Preparation for responsibilities in leadership and management
- Cross-training opportunities

resource professionals, the assessment may include discussions with management, analysis of the work done successfully by employees in similar positions, and employee surveys and focus groups. Using the results of the assessment, you can design a training program to improve individual employee skills that will contribute to overall productivity.

Orientation for New Employees

New-employee orientations have two parts: first, an introduction to company policies and procedures and second, an orientation to the employee's department, including meetings with coworkers and a review of the job description.

Behind the Numbers

HIGHER INVESTMENTS IN TRAINING

U.S. organizations are investing more in employee learning, according to a report from the American Society for Training and Development (ASTD), which used benchmark data from 281 public and private U.S. organizations of varying sizes and industries.

Average annual training expenditure per employee

Hours of formal learning

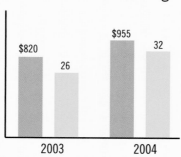

SOURCE: *2005 State of the Industry Report* by Brenda Sugrue and Ray J. Rivera (ASTD Press, 2005).

Be supportive of this orientation and reinforce its importance to the employee. New-employee training that is well planned and executed can set the right tone for your new staff member's experience at your organization and put her on the right track early on.

The BIG Picture

TRAINING AS MOTIVATION

Training programs are an opportunity to reinforce the qualities and skills that your company values in its employees. Provide a common theme or thread to the training instead of making it random and disjointed.

Provide employees with training that is completely relevant to their jobs. Use quality learning materials, hands-on experiences, and excellent instructors. Pre-session questionnaires and post-session reference materials and aids are especially helpful. Encourage employees to use their knowledge to train others.

The orientation session will be your first opportunity to expose her to the core values of your company and department and to set the stage for your work together in the years to come. Good training can even have a positive impact on morale and loyalty and reduce employee turnover.

On-the-Job Training

Two key aspects of on-the-job training are skill development and remediation. Today's workplace relies on technology to get things done.

Employees need to be comfortable with technology, from copy and fax machines to telephone systems and desktop computers. You may need to provide introductory, refresher, or advanced training in software and systems use. In addition, for some otherwise highly competent employees, you may need to provide remedial training. For instance, some workers may lack the basic skills necessary to communicate in writing.

On-the-job training can also be an excellent, informal way to broaden a person's job and

Dos & Don'ts ☑

MAKING TRAINING EFFECTIVE

Make sure training is relevant to your employees and high in quality.

☐ Do keep training practical and immediately applicable to the job.

☐ Do hire great trainers.

☐ Do break up training sessions into manageable parts.

☐ Do prepare employees beforehand for what they will learn.

☐ Don't fail to reinforce learning after the session.

☐ Don't make training a chore—be sure to position it as a privilege and opportunity for growth.

The **BIG** Picture

TRAINING AS INVESTMENT IN SUCCESS

When you add up all the costs of training, both direct and indirect, you understand why the training budget is one of the first to be slashed when times are tough.

Add the direct training charges (course fees, materials costs, instructor fees) to the indirect costs (the number of employees participating times the number of hours they are in attendance times the sum of their average hourly wages and prorated hourly cost of their benefits). The sum is not negligible.

The tangible and intangible rewards of training are hard to measure. Are people spending fewer hours producing the same amount of work? Is the quality of their work better? Has employee turnover declined? Have employees' attitudes improved? Yet training has great motivational value and builds leadership skills. And having motivated leaders at all levels of the company is a sure path to corporate success.

introduce him or her to management duties. It's a good idea to determine where employees' responsibilities can be expanded and to give them a chance periodically to make decisions more

• POWER POINTS •

ASSESSING TRAINING NEEDS

To figure out what would be best for your staff, you need a training-needs assessment with these components:

- Input from management above you
- Analysis of the work of successful employees
- Employee surveys
- Focus groups

independently or to participate in establishing priorities. You can assign employees who have leadership potential their own projects to manage, teams to lead, or other employees to supervise.

If appropriate, on-the-job training can also include cross-training—that is, instruction on how to perform different jobs within an organization, in other areas, departments, or divisions. Whether you allow employees to observe employees performing these other jobs or let them work with or be trained by their peers, this type of training can expand employees' job responsibilities and make them more versatile and more productive.

Formal Training

When employees need to improve their existing skills or learn new ones, it may be best to invest in formal training. Whether it is conducted internally or by an outside firm, formal training helps employees work up to their potential.

Formal training can be an outside seminar, a university course, or an online course. You might give employees a list of recommended business books to read and schedule times to discuss them.

Training the Trainers

Create an atmosphere of continuous learning by attending training sessions with your staff and encouraging employees to transfer their new knowledge to others. Teaching not only helps reinforce learning but also makes an employee an educational missionary. This arrangement benefits the employee, other employees, and the entire company.

REVIEWING PERFORMANCE

Many managers don't take the time to give employees adequate feedback. Some wait until an annual performance review.

If you value your people, you will make time to review their work more often. Good managers are continuously commenting on the work done by their staff members, both the good and the bad, as tasks and projects are underway or being completed.

In addition, to provide a wider perspective on employees' work and how they can improve it, good managers provide a more substantial review at least quarterly, even if the company actually requires no more than an annual review for salary adjustment purposes.

It's a good idea to develop an objective method of evaluating employees' job performance. Some companies have performance appraisal forms

> "The biggest room we have is the room for improvement. There's always something we can do better, do more often, or do with different intensity. Appropriate criticism helps us focus our attention on what we need to do to become more successful."
>
> —David Cottrell,
> author of *Monday Morning Mentoring*

with rating scales or checklists, while others permit a more narrative approach. The format you use is not as important as the information you convey to the employee and how you convey it.

Accentuate the Positive

A good performance review should be a positive learning experience, not an exercise in intimidation.

Dos & Don'ts ☑

EFFECTIVE REVIEWING

Reviewing employees is a skill that's worth developing. Good reviews can help solid employees grow into stars and ultimately make greater contributions to your work.

☐ Do provide continuous feedback.

☐ Do conduct formal reviews at least quarterly.

☐ Do use reviews to set goals for performance, skills acquisition, and advancement.

☐ Don't have someone else conduct the review of your direct report.

☐ Do give some thought to what feedback you will communicate and make notes of supporting details.

☐ Do use anonymous input from coworkers in addition to your own experience when formulating your review.

First, give employees enough notice so that they can complete a written self-appraisal and submit it to you in advance. How the employee perceives his or her performance will give you valuable insight into the individual's ability to be

☐ Do ask employees to evaluate themselves—and give them ample time to prepare.

☐ Do schedule reviews well in advance and hold them on time.

☐ Do balance negative and positive feedback.

☐ Don't fail to acknowledge specific accomplishments.

☐ Do make all criticism constructive.

☐ Don't be critical of the individual, just the behavior.

☐ Do make time for the employee to have his say.

☐ Do let employees respond in writing, if desired.

☐ Don't end one review without establishing when the next will take place.

self-critical and realistic and will help you frame your comments.

Second, make the review motivational. Always emphasize employees' strengths and praise their accomplishments. Address areas that need improvement as well, but do so constructively. Including coworkers' anonymous input—both positive and negative—is a good way to broaden the review so that it reflects more than your opinion alone.

The quarterly performance review should follow the same outline as annual reviews. This will make the annual review much easier for both you and the employee.

At the end of any performance review, employees should understand clearly what they are doing right—and what they can do better. The focus should be positive. After a review, employees should feel motivated to overcome their weaknesses rather than feel inadequate.

No Surprises

When an employee is surprised by your appraisal of his or her performance, it could be because you have not provided daily or quarterly feedback, or you have not been clear and direct in the feedback you did provide. If you have been conveying honest constructive criticism all along, then there should be no surprises.

Upward Assessments

Do you have the guts to let employees review you? Some organizations use employee surveys to rate a manager's performance. For instance, at sales meetings of Pitney Bowes, the world's largest mail specialist, the company's top managers hold forums where the salespeople—who are in the field with the customers day in and day out—rip into management strategies and policies with hard-hitting questions and confrontations. Although initially disconcerting, such "upward assessments" can have a positive impact. Managers see themselves through employees' eyes and gain new respect for the review process. Ask each employee to tell you honestly how you can do better.

CASE *FILE*

THE MORE FEEDBACK THE BETTER

Fannie Mae vice-president LeRoy Pingho realized that he wasn't getting the feedback he needed to get over what he called his "flat spots."

To rate his performance, he set up an annual review for himself—by a boss, a customer, and a subordinate. Then he wrote a report on the information he had been given, gave it to 50 people—everyone from his wife to his boss—and asked a few of them to be his "spotters." These people, with whom he worked every day, agreed to help him deal with his weaknesses. "If you see something, say something," he told them.

Having immediate feedback in an area you've targeted for improvement makes all the difference.

SOURCE: "How to Give Good Feedback" by Gina Imperato, *Fast Company* (September 1998).

Outside the Box

THE MIDDLE 70 PERCENT

Former General Electric CEO Jack Welch believes that most managers informally divide their staffs into three groups—a top-performing 20 percent who are continually rewarded for their work, the bottom 10, and the middle 70. "This middle 70 percent is enormously valuable to any company," he notes. "You simply cannot function without their skills, energy, and commitment." Keeping them motivated calls for training, positive feedback, and thoughtful goal-setting. People with promise should be cross-trained in other areas to broaden their experience and knowledge and should be given opportunity for leadership. It's not about keeping them out of the bottom 10 percent, he notes. It's about giving them the opportunity to join the top 20.

SOURCE: *Winning* by Jack Welch (Collins, 2005).

HANDLING DIFFICULT TASKS

You know about square pegs and round holes. Well, both show up in the workplace just as often as in the rest of life. Sometimes a person just can't do the job, and as a manager you are faced with the difficult task of reprimanding or even terminating him or her. Simply because most of us do not like confrontation, many managers avoid stern conversations with employees, even those who need that kind of powerful jolt to set them straight.

Part of your responsibility as a manager is to make sure your work group is functioning effectively. Consequently, if an underperforming employee is holding you back, or an employee who has trouble getting along with co-workers is disruptive, it is your responsibility to correct the situation.

When you observe an employee doing something wrong, it is important to address the issue with the employee promptly and privately. If a co-worker brings another employee's misdeed to your attention, you still need to act—but with care. Try to corroborate the story and be tactful when confronting the employee with any secondhand information.

When handling a difficult situation, it is very important to give the employee the benefit of the

• POWER POINTS •

COMMON MISTAKES

Of all the mistakes managers make in giving performance reviews, three are particularly common:

- Reviewing too infrequently
- Being underprepared
- Providing unbalanced feedback

Dos & Don'ts ☑

TAKING ACTION

Dealing with employees who don't measure up to expectations can be challenging. Here are ten keys to handling underperformers:

☐ Do deal with a difficult task as soon as it presents itself.

☐ Do remain calm and unemotional.

☐ Do provide guidance to correct the situation.

☐ Do set deadlines for required actions.

☐ Do make dated notes of every conversation and situation.

☐ Do initiate disciplinary action if the problem is not corrected.

☐ Do consider probation or termination if a problem is not resolved.

☐ Do make certain that you have just cause for oral or written reprimands and terminations.

☐ Don't attack employees personally.

☐ Don't fail to get employees to sign performance reviews and written reprimands.

doubt and to remain objective, calm, and unemotional. If your work environment has been one of mutual trust and respect, you will be better prepared to deal with any problem that comes along.

Get into the habit of documenting every problem. Make notes of who said what and when after a problem occurs and during any meetings at which it is discussed. Keep these notes in a locked file.

Reprimands

If you have been doing a good job of providing continuous feedback to your employees and reviewing their performance periodically, reprimands should rarely be necessary.

They should be issued only when there is just cause—misconduct, negligence, insubordination, unwillingness to perform job requirements, or similar circumstances.

The oral reprimand. If constructive criticism delivered in a private meeting has failed to correct an unacceptable behavior, a more official oral reprimand may be warranted. This is the first step in the progressive discipline process that may ultimately, but not necessarily, lead to termination.

In an oral reprimand, you and your employee discuss a specific problem, and you call for an action to correct it. You need to tell the employee that it is an oral reprimand, give the specific reasons behind it, and warn that a more serious consequence could result if the problem is not corrected. You should also document the oral reprimand in writing.

Plan B

CONSIDER PROBATION

Probation, a formal warning that an employee will be terminated if there is no improvement within a specified period, can help employees realize a situation's severity. It announces that they are being given one last chance.

If you opt for probation, state the reasons clearly in writing. Set a goal that is measurable and explain that termination could follow if it is not reached by a given date—usually 30, 60, or 90 days later. Ask the employee to sign the probationary notice. For some employees, this warning is all the motivation they need to improve.

The written reprimand. If the problem continues unabated, you may wish to formally put the employee on notice with a written reprimand. You must ask the employee to acknowledge the written reprimand by signing and dating a copy, and you should file a copy with your HR department. If the employee refuses to sign the reprimand, make a written note of this on your copy of the document and on the copy you send to HR.

Delivery is important. Both oral and written reprimands should be delivered privately.

WORK**FLOW** TOOLS

PROGRESSIVE DISCIPLINE STEPS

INFORMAL FEEDBACK
Given during and after
projects and tasks and
always documented in writing

PERFORMANCE REVIEWS
Given quarterly and annually

ORAL REPRIMANDS
Always given in private

WRITTEN REPRIMANDS
To be signed by employee

PROBATION
Final warning

TERMINATION
The last resort

You should also always give the employee an opportunity to respond verbally or in writing.

Whether oral or written, any reprimand must include specific references to the unacceptable behavior. You must provide thorough documentation of the nature of the behavior, when it occurred, and how it veered from acceptable standards.

Reprimanding an employee doesn't require you to be angry or upset. Stay calm even if the employee becomes emotional. Be firm yet fair in explaining the nature of the reprimand, and make it clear that additional disciplinary action could be taken if the problem is not corrected.

Delivering a reprimand is not pleasant. Don't let that deter you, however. If you have a problem on your hands that needs to be dealt with, face up to the need for the reprimand and take decisive action promptly.

Termination

Even for experienced managers, it's hard to terminate an employee. But sometimes termination is unavoidable. When a termination is due to layoffs, it can be particularly difficult, since it may come as a surprise to the employee.

When termination is the result of poor performance, it is not necessarily easier, but at least the employee should not be shocked if you have provided regular feedback in the form of constructive criticism and performance reviews. To prepare for a termination, thorough written documentation of past unresolved problems is essential. If you have any doubt, you need only review your paperwork to be certain that you are justified in taking action. Be sure you know your company's policy on termination and the provisions of federal and state laws.

"It's awful to fire people. But if you have a candid organization with clear performance expectations and a performance evaluation process . . . then people in the bottom 10 percent generally know who they are. When you tell them, they usually leave before you ask them to."

—Jack Welch, former CEO of General Electric

Whatever the reason for the termination, deliver the news calmly and objectively. Although the meeting should be private, it may be appropriate to have an HR representative present.

Dos & Don'ts ☑

TERMINATION

Firing someone is never easy. But knowing the protocols can help the process go more smoothly.

- ☐ Do create a paper trail. Keep written, dated accounts of any incidents or problems that occur.

- ☐ Don't terminate an employee without complete documentation.

- ☐ Do plan what you are going to say at the termination meeting. Practice if necessary.

- ☐ Don't berate the employee during the termination meeting.

- ☐ Do gather information about unemployment, health insurance, severance, and other benefits.

An employee's reaction can run the gamut from disbelief to anger to tears. Show compassion but be firm. Make it clear that the decision is final. Your objective is to terminate the employee without impugning his or her dignity.

Former General Electric CEO Jack Welch, widely considered one of the century's most influential business leaders, says that what you do after you fire someone matters as much

- [ ] Do bring a termination letter to the meeting that details severance details.

- [ ] Do prepare a checklist of what the employee must turn in before leaving.

- [ ] Do treat the employee respectfully and stay calm and unemotional.

- [ ] Do block access to e-mail and telephone as soon as the employee leaves.

- [ ] Do not let a terminated employee leave with confidential information.

- [ ] Do notify remaining employees about the termination as soon as you can.

- [ ] Do not retract a termination once you have made the decision.

as how you do it. Specifically, don't let your employee feel that he's a pariah. Even if you are angry, you have to bolster his self-esteem and assure him that he will find another job that's a better match. It's possible that the lead for that job could come from you. A soft landing for him is your objective. "Every person who leaves goes on to represent your company," Welch notes. "They can bad-mouth or they can praise."

Essential Skill II
Managing Teams

"Teamwork is the ability to work together toward a common vision. The ability to direct individual accomplishments toward organizational objectives. It is the fuel that allows common people to attain uncommon results."

—Andrew Carnegie,
philanthropist and founder
of Carnegie Steel Company
(1835–1919)

Why work in teams? To put it simply, you'll accomplish more—and do it more efficiently. The modern workplace is leaner, and managers are expected to do more with less. The properly managed team can produce more work of better quality, faster, than individuals working alone.

A team doesn't exist to give its members the pleasure of teamwork. Whether the team is a work group team, a sales team, or a service team, it exists to accomplish something specific, and its members share a common sense of purpose. The old saying "The whole is greater than the sum of its parts" is never truer than for a team.

Good teams are grounded in collaboration and cooperation. The culture of the workplace must embrace the concept of working together; you must embrace being a team leader.

Team leadership involves doing four things well: building your team, defining the roles of

The BIG Picture

TEAMS ACCOMPLISH AMAZING THINGS

In his book *Creativity*, author Mihaly Csikszentmihalyi points out that in Florence, between 1400 and 1425, five different artists created five of the most celebrated works in all of art history.

- Filippo Brunelleschi designed the cathedral dome.

- Lorenzo Ghiberti sculpted the Gates of Paradise.

- Donatello created sculptures in the chapel of Orsanmichele.

- Masaccio painted frescoes in the Brancacci Chapel.

your team members, motivating your team, and using your team effectively.

BUILDING TEAMS

Managers who don't inherit teams must start with existing employees. Rarely do you have the opportunity to build a new team from the ground up. Even so, you can make an impact by conveying a sense of purpose and direction.

Define the Team's Role

It falls to you as the manager and team leader to spell out what the team is expected to accomplish.

- Gentile da Fabriano rendered the "Adoration of the Magi" in the Church of the Trinity.

This was more than just coincidence, he believes. The collaboration of the artists with their patrons, and the feedback these patrons gave during the creation of each work, pushed the artists to heights that they might never have achieved on their own. In other words, outstanding performance is never a solo accomplishment.

SOURCE: *Executive Intelligence* by Justin Menkes (Collins, 2005).

Make the goal specific and measurable; it can be as ambitious as you need it to be, but it should still be realistic. Set a deadline.

At the same time, explain how the team's work supports the goals of your organization as a whole. Often, when people work closely on a team, their perspective becomes narrower and more focused. Although this changed perspective helps them do their work, knowing the bigger picture is important in making decisions and maintaining enthusiasm for the tasks at hand. In addition, make a point of consistently reminding your group of the value of their efforts.

Know Your Team Members

Chances are that not all team members are equally committed to the team—or equally competent.

• POWER POINTS •

MANAGING TEAMS

Working in teams is a way for managers to accomplish more with less. These are the basic principles for managing teams:

- A team exists to accomplish something.

- Teams are built on cooperation and collaboration.

- Team leaders know how to build and motivate teams and use them effectively.

CASE *FILE*

A WHOLE CULTURE OF TEAMS

Whole Foods has become one of the most successful natural foods grocery retailers. One major reason, according to cofounder and CEO John Mackey, is its team culture.

Each store operates on its own with an average of ten teams managing the store's departments. The teams have leaders and performance targets.

Whole Foods promotes the concept of internal competition. Each store's teams, the stores themselves, and the company's regions compete with one another. Bonuses, recognition, and promotions are directly tied to superior performance.

It makes for a whole company of teams focused on excellence.

SOURCE: "Whole Foods Is All Teams" by Charles Fishman, *Fast Company* (April/May 1996).

As team leader, you need to learn which is which, to determine the strengths and talents of each person, and to make appropriate assignments. If you have the option, choose employees with complementary skills. Some employees may be better suited to certain tasks than others. Some may show initiative; others need more support.

Dos & Dont's ☑

RECOGNIZING INDIVIDUALITY

When managing a team, start by viewing each team member as unique.

☐ Do match team members' roles to their individual capabilities.

☐ Don't force people into roles for which they're ill-suited.

☐ Do make organized, detail-oriented individuals your administrators and project managers.

☐ Do assign your creative people the job of generating ideas. They are the ones who will spark the team to think inventively.

☐ Do try to find someone with subject-matter expertise.

☐ Do designate a social, outgoing team member as your team builder.

☐ Do make sure everyone understands everyone else's role.

Training may be required for some to reach the standards set for the group—or the team as a whole may need instruction.

Foster Cooperation

Teams succeed only when their members cooperate closely and work collaboratively. However, not everyone is capable of that. While it's necessary to respect different personalities, as a team leader you cannot let personality differences impede your progress. You need to reinforce

> "I've always found that the speed of the boss is the speed of the team."
>
> —Lee Iacocca,
> former CEO of Chrysler

mutual respect, cooperation, and teamwork. Praise team members for collaborating. Encourage the open sharing of information.

At times, you may have to mediate differences between team members. Even as you encourage independent thinking, be sure that the end result makes a contribution to the team's goals.

Build Team Spirit

The work of a team can be intense at times. In the best teams, the shared experience of working towards a goal—with all the advances and setbacks that entails—creates a strong sense of camaraderie.

However, this team spirit takes time to develop. At the beginning, you can help moderate the mood by having team members share something

Dos & Dont's ☑

HOW TO BUILD STRONG TEAMS

An effective team can accomplish more than any single individual. The better you are at managing teams, the better your results will be.

☐ Do define what you want accomplished before you start building your team.

☐ Do explain the team's purpose—don't assume members understand it.

☐ Do explain how success will be measured.

☐ Do consider members' unique strengths and weaknesses when assigning roles to team members.

personal at your meetings. Occasionally use team-building exercises. Get the team together socially—out to dinner, to a sporting event, or on a hike. In other words, have some fun.

Then, when you create team T-shirts, sweatshirts, baseball hats, pens, or coffee mugs, the team slogan or icon members display will become powerful reminders of the team's shared experiences, both achievements and setbacks, and your common goal. These logo items will become one more way of reminding the group that they are part of something important.

- ☐ Do provide appropriate training—for individuals or for the group as a whole.

- ☐ Do foster collaboration and cooperation.

- ☐ Don't let personality differences and conflicts impede team progress.

- ☐ Do nurture and promote team spirit.

- ☐ Do set a high standard for team performance.

- ☐ Do monitor team progress.

- ☐ Don't abdicate responsibility for the results.

Insist on Accountability

A team is not a place for employees to avoid responsibility. Set high performance standards, and expect each team member to make an effort to contribute. Empower team members to be self-sufficient, but always be available to guide them. Even if you promote consensus decision-making, you are ultimately accountable for the team's success. For that reason, monitor your team diligently. Make sure team members leave progress meetings knowing what is expected and feeling accountable for getting it done.

CASE *FILE*

HOW DO TEAMS AFFECT A BUSINESS?

To find out, economics professor Derek C. Jones and his colleague Takao Kato spent 35 months doing in-depth interviews and surveys and even shadowing workers at a fast-growing light manufacturing firm that makes parts for other businesses.

The CEO of the multinational company that owned the firm believed in teams and had initiated a teaming program throughout the manufacturing plant.

When Jones and Kato analyzed individual team members' daily output of parts, the number rejected because of poor quality, and the number of "downtime" hours consumed by

DEFINING ROLES ON TEAMS

It's important to realize that the team you build is made up of people, each of whom has unique skills, experience, capabilities, and talents. A smart manager who wants to build a successful team assesses each individual's strengths and leverages them to maximum advantage in service of the team's goals.

In their best-selling book, *First, Break All the Rules* (Simon & Schuster, 1999), Marcus Buckingham and Curt Coffman make the point that it is far more effective to focus on each individual's strengths and to

nonproduction-related job activities, the findings were startling. Initially, individual productivity among team members increased significantly—by about 3 percent—and rejection rates dropped more than 25 percent.

In fact, for those whom management had invited to join the teams, the overall benefits were lasting. And these statistics measure only the team membership's impact on the productivity of individual workers, apart from workplace improvements the teams had developed.

SOURCE: "The Effects of Employee Involvement on Firm Performance" by Derek C. Jones and Takao Kato, The William Davidson Institute (September 2003).

cultivate his or her talents than to make an attempt to remediate his or her weaknesses. The authors encourage all managers to "help each person become more and more of who he already is."

The authors suggest that many managers are more comfortable with assumptions and generalizations about types of people, such as "ego-driven salespeople" or "shy accountants," rather than dealing with the reality that each person is different.

GOOD WORKS

Companies can use team building not only to reach their corporate goals but also to promote global citizenship.

Dell's Global Community Involvement Week encouraged employees around the world to contribute time, energy, and enthusiasm to help the global community. In the United States, 52 teams represented 2,500 employees and Dell teams in 16 countries spearheaded community service efforts during a designated seven-day period. Thousands of Dell team members engaged in community service activities ranging from educational fairs to building houses.

Dell has numerous other team-building programs. The Team Building Match Grant Program, for example, encourages departmental and team building by providing a financial match to a not-for-profit organization chosen as a beneficiary by a Dell employee team.

SOURCE: Dell, Inc., www.dell.com.

THE BOTTOM LINE

Find the Difference

Make the extra effort to develop a thorough understanding of the capabilities of your team members. Then use that insight to put people in the right team roles.

Do you have someone on your team who is organized and detail-oriented—perhaps someone with project management experience? This person could be well suited to be the team's administrator. An administrator helps coordinate individual team members' efforts, keeps work on schedule, tracks the status of tasks, minds the details, and so on.

The BIG Picture

THE INTANGIBLE IMPACT OF TEAMS

An us-versus-them mentality pervades in many workplaces. Sometimes this division between employees and their managers is reinforced by company policy and traditions, and sometimes it exists as a subtle undercurrent. It is anathema to the team spirit.

However, a strong team philosophy can make a positive impact that counters this mentality. Even as a leader, when you participate as a team member, you join employees on common ground—and you're all on the same side.

Is there a team member who is always coming up with ideas or has a creative side but isn't very organized? This person might be the team's idea-generator, someone who functions as a "spark plug" and gets the team thinking broadly and imaginatively.

Does one of your team members have expertise in a subject, or in-depth knowledge of a system or process that might be of value to the team? This person could be the team subject-matter expert, the person others rely on for information and facts.

Is one of your team members particularly social and outgoing? This person might function as a

EIGHT INGREDIENTS OF PERFORMANCE

In his classic book, *The Wisdom of Teams,* Jon Katzenbach says there's no perfect recipe for building team performance. However, his research has illuminated eight ingredients that most high-performance teams shared.

- Management imparts a sense of urgency and sets a clear direction.
- Team members are selected based on skills and potential, not personalities.
- First-time interactions of the team members are positive.

liaison to other teams or take the responsibility for setting up team-building exercises and events.

Formalize the Roles

Once you've matched the individuals with their roles, formalize these roles. If you have more roles to fill than you have team members, some members will need to take on multiple roles. This is not uncommon among smaller teams; you should still be able to accomplish your goals.

Define each of the roles as specifically as possible. What tasks must be accomplished? What are the dependencies of one role to another? Is it necessary for the responsibilities of one role

- Management has set clear rules of behavior.
- Immediate performance-oriented tasks and goals have been laid out.
- The group has been challenged with new perspectives and information.
- The group spends a considerable amount of time together.
- Management exploits the power of positive feedback, recognition, and rewards.

SOURCE: *The Wisdom of Teams* by Jon R. Katzenbach and Douglas K. Smith (Harvard Business School Press, 1992).

THE BOTTOM LINE

to be completed before another role begins? Be sure that individual team members know not only their own roles but also those of other team members. This is one situation in which it's good for everyone to know each other's business.

Set the Course

Once all your team members know their own roles and each other's, get everyone together to determine what needs to be done and when. They must take ownership of the process, begin to function cooperatively, and collaborate to complete the

> "A team is a living aggregation of individual talent. Sure, its collective capabilities may add up to more than the sum of the parts. But if we forget to nurture and cultivate each part, the sum can never achieve greatness."
>
> —Frank Pacetta,
> author of *Stop Whining—and Start Winning*

assigned tasks. Have your administrator provide a schedule that shows what needs to be done, when, and by whom. Jump-start the work with a meeting to review roles and reiterate your goals.

Dos & Dont's ☑

HOW TO KEEP A TEAM STRONG

Personalities are apt to clash and tempers to flare when a team is at work. Try to prevent the resulting tensions from affecting your team's progress.

☐ Don't support one team member over another when conflicts arise.

☐ Do make an effort to be impartial in resolving disagreements.

☐ Don't harshly criticize any team member in front of others.

☐ Don't favor one employee over another in distributing team rewards.

☐ Do encourage all team members to voice their opinions honestly.

☐ Don't expect every team member to be equally committed.

☐ Do work to communicate a strong answer to the inevitable question, "What's in it for me?"

MOTIVATING TEAMS

It sounds paradoxical, but motivating a team starts with motivating individuals.

While it is nice to think that people want to work together in teams just to be more productive, they are motivated by self-interest. They expect to be personally rewarded for their efforts.

Each and every team member wants to feel important. Each individual's self-esteem needs to be affirmed. Each needs an appealing answer to the question "What's in it for me?"

You can provide the answer by making sure individuals understand that their collective effort will bring benefits they would not enjoy if they were working alone—not so much salary increases and promotions as other distinct rewards and benefits.

Working as One

Demonstrate by your attitude, actions, and words that your staff's work as a unified team is important to you and to the organization you all work for. Make a point of reinforcing this message at every team meeting, in all team communications, and whenever you set goals and review progress.

Make it fun to work as one. Create a team logo or saying with your team members. Put it on team memos and paraphernalia.

Show team members that you expect them to work as a team and promise to reward them for doing so. Motivate them even more by telling them that the team's rewards will increase as the team's performance increases.

Outside the Box

LEARN BY ROLE-PLAYING

One novel way to encourage team members to respect each others' roles is to conduct a role-playing exercise.

In it, encourage team members to switch roles and act out how they might handle specific situations or problems. Have two team members who switch roles "perform" in front of the other team members. The other team members should comment on what they observe.

Role-playing can be a valuable learning experience for the entire team. Be sure to be impartial when conducting this exercise.

Motivational Exercises and Events

Consider using icebreakers and motivational exercises at the beginning of team meetings and at other team events. Such exercises promote camaraderie and help team members get to know one another better. Exercises might include presentations, skits, drawing, writing, or some other form of interaction. Develop exercises that are appropriate to your company and your team.

Motivational events can also help make the team more cohesive. Parties, excursions, tours, and other group events are other options worth considering. Some companies endorse the use

• POWER POINTS •

TIME FOR REWARDS

Individual motivators vary—monetary rewards work for some and non-monetary rewards work for others. Make the point that working as a team can be rewarding by offering various creative incentives:

- Bonuses

- Profit-sharing

- Stock options

- Team excursions

- Hats, mugs, team items

- Parties

- Prizes such as lessons, health-club memberships, and tickets to events

- Seminars and conventions

- Vacations and weekend trips

- Certificates, plaques, ribbons, and medals, publicly displayed

- Public acknowledgment of team accomplishments in a newsletter or memo or at a meeting

of ropes courses and Outward Bound–style programs to heighten team motivation.

Material Rewards

Incentives such as prizes, vacations, bonuses, profit-sharing, or stock options can dramatize the point that working as a team can be rewarding. However, be sure to distinguish team rewards from individual rewards. Having team members share a bonus pool that increases as the team meets specific objectives is different from rewarding an individual salesperson who exceeds her sales quota. Any team reward should be distributed equitably, so as not to favor one employee over another.

> "If you want star players, reward the stars. If you want star teams, reward team players."
>
> —James B. Miller, corporate coach

A department, division, or company profit-sharing program is a good example of a team-oriented monetary reward. Typically, a profit-sharing program distributes payments to employees based on the successful achievement of one of its financial objectives. Since all employees contribute to that goal, each one will be eligible to receive some portion of the profit. Sometimes this portion is based on time with the company or seniority in the corporate hierarchy. Profit-sharing motivates the individual to work on behalf of the larger team to get the maximum financial reward.

USING TEAMS EFFECTIVELY

Your direction as a manager is one of the keys to your team's effectiveness. It is your responsibility to set goals, monitor progress, and establish criteria for success. But it's equally important that you solicit and applaud your team's input in these areas so that each team member feels a part of the process.

> "As a leader, your job is to gently steer the team toward a more useful direction and toward solutions, and then let them do the thinking."
>
> —David Rock,
> author of *Quiet Leadership*

There are two ways to provide direction to your team. The first is to meet with individual team members whenever they need guidance, have a problem, or are experiencing conflicts with another team member.

The second is to convene team meetings when you have a specific agenda or want to monitor the team's progress. To keep these meetings efficient, establish what you want to accomplish and set a time limit at the outset. Share the purpose of the meeting with team members in advance. Invite the smallest possible number of people without arbitrarily excluding team members.

Red Flags ✕◆

WARNING SIGNS OF DIVISION

Watch out for these signals that a team is not unified:

- **Lack of direction** – The team is unsure of its purpose or goal.

- **Team malaise** – Team members seem to lack energy and spirit.

- **Frequent flare-ups** – Two or more team members seem to be often at odds.

- **Decision paralysis** – The team is unable to reach a decision together.

- **Incompatibility** – One or more team members ask to be transferred to another team.

• POWER POINTS •

THE SELF-MANAGED TEAM

A self-managed team can accomplish a great deal if the manager steps back and lets the team succeed. Self-managed teams thrive when:

- The members of the team feel empowered.

- Team members have some authority to make decisions.

- Team members take on expanded roles and responsibilities.

- A coach, not a supervisor, is at the helm.

Resolving Conflict

It is almost inevitable that tempers will flare between team members at some point. This is not at all unusual when people work closely together under deadlines.

It is best if conflicting team members can work out their differences without your intervention; however, any conflict has the potential to disable the effectiveness of the team. When you become aware of a conflict, meet with the team members who are involved individually first and then, if necessary, together. Reinforce the importance of working together as a team and try to facilitate a resolution.

Empowering the Team

The most effective teams are those whose members feel empowered. Efficiency is high. The individuals work together like a well-oiled machine, each one accepting responsibility for the success of the team as a whole. Not only do team members accomplish tasks on schedule, they also practice consensus decision-making.

For this situation to develop, the team needs to be given a certain amount of authority to function independently and make decisions.

Plan B

TEAM TIME-OUT

If a team is either always at odds or chronically underperforming, it may be time for a team reality check.

Get everyone together for a frank and honest discussion. The group might need to hear what the consequences will be if they continue to fail to meet team goals.

Probe to find out whether team members feel responsible and accountable for the team's success. Remind the group that if they miss their goals, they won't earn the rewards that are due to the team.

Often these steps can get the team back on track.

Dos & Dont's ☑

HELP YOUR TEAM BECOME EFFECTIVE

As the team leader, you can have a significant impact on the success of your team.

☐ Don't abdicate your responsibility for monitoring the team's progress.

☐ Don't hold team meetings without a specific agenda.

☐ Don't allow conflicts to continue if you believe they are affecting the team's effectiveness.

☐ Do get out of the way if your team members already accept individual responsibility for the team's success.

☐ Don't micromanage a team that already functions effectively.

Not all team members are comfortable with this responsibility. In fact, team members of such a self-managed team often find that their jobs expand and they need to take on new, broader responsibilities.

Still, self-managed teams can accomplish a great deal. If you put into practice the strategies and techniques discussed earlier, it is quite possible to build a self-managed team. Consider yourself lucky if you do. When a self-managed team becomes truly successful, an interesting thing happens: the manager becomes not so much a supervisor as a coach. Your role is no less important, but it is certainly different.

The best course of action, when possible, is to get out of the way and let the team succeed. Be available to answer questions and offer guidance. Be a sounding board. Facilitate decision-making when the need arises. Monitor progress.

Don't completely let go of the rudder, but don't overmanage your team if it is capable of getting the work done on its own. After all, it is a tribute to you as a manager when such an effective team hits its stride.

Essential Skill III
Managing Projects

"How do you know when your project measures up? Each week, ask, "Will we be bragging about this project five years from now? Never let a project go dreary on you."

—Tom Peters

Managing projects takes the skills you acquire managing people and teams and applies them to a deliverable. A project is any deliverable—a report, a presentation, a strategic plan, a manufactured product—for which you have management responsibility.

Typically, managing a project means managing three components—resources, money, and time—that are separate but interdependent and, taken together, comprise the scope of the project.

THE PROJECT'S SCOPE

In effect, the scope of the project is what you need to accomplish with the resources, money, and time you have available. Most project management experts say that properly defining the scope of the project at the outset is the ingredient most critical to its success.

To define the scope, you need to fully understand the nature of the project, its objective, and what you think will be required to get it done. Can the project legitimately be accomplished

• POWER POINTS •

WHAT'S A PROJECT?

A project is any deliverable for which you have management responsibility. The three critical elements are:

- **Resources** – People, equipment, physical material, outside services

- **Money** – Funds allocated for the project, anticipated profit

- **Time** – How long it takes to reach each milestone and to complete the project overall

WORK **FLOW** TOOLS

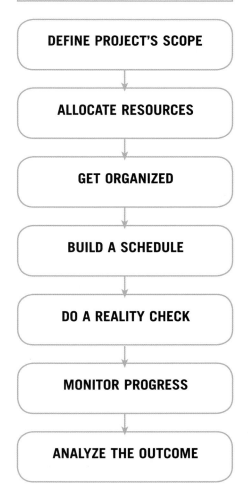

BASIC PROJECT MANAGEMENT

DEFINE PROJECT'S SCOPE

ALLOCATE RESOURCES

GET ORGANIZED

BUILD A SCHEDULE

DO A REALITY CHECK

MONITOR PROGRESS

ANALYZE THE OUTCOME

CASE *FILE*

STRONG PLANS ARE TOP PERFORMERS

For Washington Group International, a large engineering consulting firm, weak project management is not an option. The company runs projects in 30 countries at any given time—as many as 400 to 500 jobs at once.

Not only does repeat business depend on successful execution of every project, but so do the firm's earnings: Revenues from most of the contracts are linked to performance. Consequently, successful execution of every project has a direct impact on the bottom line.

With this impetus, the firm has learned that projects with a well-defined planning process and strong execution plans outperform projects with weaker plans by five to one. Strong project management skills are a firm value and part of its corporate culture. As a result, about 75 percent of the firm's jobs meet or exceed targeted performance due to project management, according to Tom Zarges, executive vice president of operations.

SOURCE: "Beyond the Bottom Line" by Marla Schulman, *PM Network* (January 2005).

with the available resources, money, and time? What is the budget? The delivery date? Are there elements of the project that you believe should be *outside* the project's scope? A project's scope is dynamic—it should change if the project is modified along the way.

PRACTICE MAKES PERFECT

The more mature an organization's project management practices, the more likely the organization will reach a high level of performance. A 2006 survey of senior practitioners indicated that improving the level of project management maturity, assessed via an industry standard model, has a direct impact on performance benefits.

The most significant difference between high-performing and low-performing organizations is in their allocation of resources and their estimates of what they will need to see a project through successfully from beginning to end.

High-performing organizations are also significantly better at completing projects on schedule.

SOURCE: *Project Management Maturity* (The Center for Business Practices, 2006).

THE BOTTOM LINE

Dos & Dont's ☑

AVOID COMMON MISTAKES

Planning carefully, then managing projects closely as they change, is crucial.

☐ Don't assume all projects are the same; each one has its own requirements and challenges.

☐ Don't take shortcuts in the project management process.

☐ Do plan for contingencies; the scope of most projects changes as they progress.

☐ Do understand that a change of scope is a failure only if you did not plan for it or communicate the change to others.

Your job is to determine what changes in scope may be needed—in terms of more or fewer resources, money, or time—if the project changes.

Managing projects closely is key. Sometimes the project may not appear to change dramatically. However, several seemingly insignificant changes can occur that, when added up, contribute to a phenomenon known as "scope creep." Suddenly, the project you're managing seems to be consuming more resources, time, or money. This is when you need to stop to assess the project and possibly make a scope change.

A scope change implies that additional resources, money, or time will be needed for the project. Once you decide a scope change is required, you will likely need to gain approval before going any further.

Goals and Objectives Defined

For any project to reach its successful completion, the manager and project team must understand the project's goals and objectives. These two terms are often confused, but they represent very different concepts.

A project goal describes the broader aim of the project, often in the context of a business goal. Goals are expressed in general terms and are not typically measurable.

The objective of a project, on the other hand, relates to the specific outcome desired from the project. Objectives are usually expressed in concrete terms, typically using numbers, percentages, and other measurable terms.

Here is an example. Suppose a university is embarking on a major capital project to improve its library. One of the goals of the project is to help improve the reputation of the university as a research institution on a national level. One of the objectives of the project is to add enough physical capacity by autumn of 2008 to increase the library's book holdings from 50,000 to 100,000 volumes.

It is important for a manager to understand the project goal, but it is *essential* for a manager to live the project objective. Objectives represent real, measurable results. The objective is what you, as a manager, have been tasked to achieve. The degree to which your objective is achieved will be the basis for your evaluation as a project manager.

About Goals and Objectives

Goals for a project should always be tied to business goals. A definable project does not exist in a vacuum—its reason for being is to support a larger business goal. In fact, a project may fulfill only a portion of a goal; it may take several projects to meet a particular goal.

Project objectives can be set by project managers, with the approval of senior management.

Dos & Dont's ☑

HOW TO SET GOALS AND OBJECTIVES

To a great extent, the success of a project is determined in the initial phases, with the establishment of the goals and objectives.

- ☐ Don't confuse goals and objectives.

- ☐ Do create objectives that describe the specific outcome of the project.

- ☐ Do get the project team involved in setting the objectives.

- ☐ Don't allow others to set objectives without your approval for projects that you will be responsible for managing.

However, it's also wise to involve a project's team members in setting objectives, since they will be doing the work. The objectives will be more readily achievable if the team wholeheartedly embraces the objectives of the project up front.

Involving the team does not mean leaving the final decision to the group, however. Although you want to encourage the members of your team to participate in setting objectives, it should be up to you as the project manager to make the final decision. It is ultimately the success of the group in meeting the objective you've established that will be measured.

☐ Do establish criteria at the outset for measuring results, if need be.

☐ Don't set project objectives that you know are unrealistic or too aggressive.

☐ Do accept that it may take several projects to meet a particular goal.

☐ Do make sure that your goals describe the broader aim of the project and are in keeping with business goals.

☐ Do take final responsibility yourself for achieving the objective.

The easiest way to set an objective is to understand what the project must accomplish. A project is generally designed to change or improve something. The objective expresses a desired improvement, in terms of resources, time, or money. The objective should be realistic and achievable.

In addition, criteria should be established so that the project's results can be accurately measured. You need to be able to impartially evaluate whether or not the project is meeting its objective.

Managing Project Milestones

As a manager, you should also establish project milestones—deliverables or checkpoints that occur at specified intervals on the project's critical path. By reaching these mini-objectives on schedule, you and your team know that the project is on track. Missing a milestone can have a snowball effect on the entire project. Consequently, managing milestones is one way to keep a project on track and ultimately meet the project's objectives.

It is important to note that project milestones may or may not be dependent on one another. Often there are constraints on resources, time, or money so that milestones cannot occur strictly in sequence. Some parts of the project may have to be done concurrently, and tasks may well overlap.

In such cases, you may feel as if you have many balls in the air at once as you manage the project. It takes a competent team of individuals with

Dos & Dont's ☑

MILESTONES MATTER

Once you've set your goals and objectives, it's important to establish the deliverables or checkpoints that will occur along the way. Here's what to keep in mind:

☐ Do involve your project team when deciding on task checkpoints.

☐ Do have team members manage their individual portions of the project.

☐ Don't fail to manage major milestones yourself.

☐ Don't expect all milestones to be reached sequentially—some may have to be concurrent.

☐ Do take advantage of project management software to help you plan and manage milestones.

clearly defined responsibilities to make sure your critical milestones are reached on time.

Quality, Time, and Money

Often, a project goal is to improve quality in some measurable way. A typical project objective is to do that on time and within a specified budget.

Quality, time, and money form a triangular relationship in the project management world.

Many experts believe you can optimally achieve only two out of three in any project: You can't obtain the highest quality in the shortest time frame at the lowest cost.

From a practical perspective, every project has some budgetary and scheduling constraints, so the real issue becomes the definition of "quality." Quality, says the American Society for Quality, comprises the characteristics of a product or service "that bear on its ability to satisfy stated or implied needs."

Dos & Dont's ☑

THE SEARCH FOR QUALITY

Be sure to define the quality you want from your project from the outset.

☐ Do recognize that the definition of "quality" can vary from project to project.

☐ Do quantify the improvement in quality you're seeking if you want to make it a project objective.

☐ Do estimate the time and money it might take to achieve a quality-improvement objective.

☐ Don't accept an inadequate timeline or budget in a quality-improvement project without negotiating for a modified objective or an increase in the timeline and budget.

If a project goal is to improve quality, then the manager must gain some guidance as to how to quantify the improvement. If it can be quantified, then a specific quality improvement objective can be set.

The next question is what kind of time and money it takes to achieve this improvement. Although you can strive to meet the defined objective, it may not ultimately be attainable if the schedule and budget are inadequate. If you have the knowledge and experience to foresee the shortfall at the outset, you can collaborate with your own managers to redefine the scope of the project.

Red Flags ✖

POOR PROJECT PLANNING

When there is a breakdown in planning, project objectives are less likely to be achieved. Watch out for:

- **A poorly defined scope** – This starts a project off on the wrong foot.

- **Scope creep** – Unwanted surprises pop up if you disregard small scope changes, and a project can spin out of control.

- **Inadequate resource allocation** – A project can run aground if the manpower, funds, and time alloted are insufficient.

DEFINING THE PROCESS

Projects in today's business world are increasingly complex. In addition, expectations for completing projects have become more and more aggressive. Businesses need to accomplish more in less time and within tighter budgets.

Although some managers believe in managing projects informally, there is a growing awareness that most projects require a certain discipline to bring together the necessary project elements and execute the project within budget and on time. This process is fairly standard and extends across

CASE *FILE*

A LAW FIRM TAKES CONTROL

With more than 1,000 attorneys, Foley & Lardner LLP needed a system to schedule, track, and report on projects—one that was easy to implement and maintain.

Rather than adopt software already available in the marketplace, the firm decided to develop a brand new system for project management. It has dramatically changed the way the firm manages projects.

Throughout the firm, project managers create and track projects using a single methodology, and executives can check project status online and obtain detailed information about how the project is progressing.

many types of projects, varying only with the complexity of the project and its components.

Scope. Determine the precise scope of the project. You need to spell out ahead of time what you need to accomplish with the resources, money, and time you have available.

Resource allocation. Determine what inside staff, outside resources, physical material, equipment, and other items will be needed to execute the project.

Organization. Plan how you will work on the project and choose the right people for each task. Explain the project objective to your group, and get everyone pointed in the right direction.

The result? Project managers are more productive, the firm has reduced costs for itself and its clients, and up-to-date information about any project in any office is now readily available to all authorized users.

Developing the new system "forced us to come up with a unified project management process," says a project manager at Foley & Lardner. "This has made us more productive. Where it used to take 20 hours to create a project schedule, now, with the new project templates, I can do it in four or five hours."

SOURCE: "Foley & Lardner LLP: Law Firm Improves Project Management Processes, Boosts Productivity," www.microsoft.com (June 19, 2005).

Outside the Box

CONSIDER FLEXIBLE DEVELOPMENT

When you create a process to manage a project, structure without constraint is always a goal. You need a structure so that everyone knows what comes next and your progress can be measured. But you can't underestimate the impact of changes along the way. Change is fairly likely in many situations, sometimes because the market for your product is volatile, sometimes because of management changes in your company.

You need to plan for the change from the outset and make project decisions in a way that leaves you wiggle room in case of snafus.

Specialists in project management have developed a methodology to handle this type of situation in an organized way that aims to minimize the excess cost and impact of changes, a process called "flexible development." Consultants in the field can help you design a custom system as well as educate you, via private or public seminars, in the approach.

SOURCE: "Developing Products on 'Internet Time'" by Alan MacCormack et al., *Management Science* (January 2001).

Scheduling. Set your start and end dates. Map out all the other milestones for the project from beginning to end. Include target dates for the completion of these milestone tasks that, in combination, will meet the final end date required for the project. Get the members of your team involved in determining milestones for their individual tasks and functions.

> "The better work men do is always done under stress and at great personal cost."
> —William Carlos Williams,
> American poet
> (1883–1963)

Reality check. Rethink all the details to make sure that your schedule is realistic and that your resources and budget seem adequate. If you suspect that the objectives are unrealistic for the resources you have, ask for more—money or time—or negotiate for a modified objective. Planning for contingencies early on can save you from disaster later.

Tracking progress. Manage your team, monitor the schedule, and keep written reports on progress. Carefully document any scope changes, then inform management and get changes approved as required. It is almost inevitable that some parts of your project will not go as planned.

Analysis of the outcome. A project isn't completely finished until you review and assess how it was executed and managed and whether it successfully met its objectives.

The Right Tools

The right project management tools can minimize risk and help assure that a project will reach a successful conclusion.

Project management software is one such tool. Project management software can help you scope a project, schedule milestones, and estimate time, money, and resources. It can also help you manage all these elements continuously so that you can stay on top of scope changes, deadlines, and estimated-versus-actual requirements.

Project management software can also help facilitate communication about the project. Whether you use e-mail, written reports, staff meetings, or a combination of all these, it is essential to communicate updates or changes in the project's status to both team members and company management on an ongoing basis.

The right tools can also help you standardize project management practices. If typical projects in your organization are fully documented, you will have the ability to study these projects, compare them to the project you need to complete, and see in advance what the scope included, how resources were managed, what issues came up,

The **BIG** Picture

COMPANIES RATE THEIR SYSTEMS

When asked to rate the maturity level of their project management systems, most companies say they are not satisfied, according to the first global survey on the subject, undertaken by PriceWaterhouseCoopers.

Interestingly, the survey showed that while senior management tended to blame project managers for poor results, the true reasons for failures lay in imbalances within the organization that was undertaking the project—situations that were clearly outside the direct influence of the managers of those projects.

The survey also found that failures in project management tend to take place more often in organizations with a lower level of project management maturity. Lower maturity means project management is not institutionalized and processes are informal.

Staff development and professional certification have a positive impact on minimizing project failures—and raising an organization's project maturity level.

SOURCE: "Boosting Performance through Programme in Project Management," PriceWaterhouseCoopers, www.pwc.com.

what unanticipated problems arose—and how each of these situations was handled. This will greatly increase your ability to complete your project successfully.

> "It is well known that 'problem avoidance' is an important part of problem solving. Instead of solving the problem, you go upstream and alter the system so that the problem does not occur in the first place."
>
> —Edward de Bono,
> motivational author

Assessing and Managing Risk

An element of risk hovers over every project. The potential for problems due to inadequate resources, budget over-runs, missed deadlines, do-overs, or the inexperience of team members is obvious.

Battle-tested project managers assess the potential snafus early in the game, before they derail the project. Risk analysis is often based

Behind the Numbers

TROUBLED PROJECTS

In a recent survey, senior practitioners with knowledge of their organizations' management practices characterized 47 percent of their projects as "troubled," "troubled and recovered," or "troubled and failed." Out of 3,874 projects that closed in a 12-month period, 1,830 were troubled.

Only 24 percent of the organizations surveyed had a standard process for recovering troubled projects, and 31 percent had no process at all. Organizations with a standard recovery process had more successful projects by 83 percent.

SOURCE: *Troubled Projects* (Center for Business Practices, 2006).

on the execution of similar projects. Sometimes project team members and managers discuss possible problems, document their findings, and develop preventive strategies.

This is a smart way to keep projects under control. Taking the time early on to anticipate what could go wrong later is worth the effort. It lets you plan for contingencies—to build a schedule loose enough to accommodate potential delays, for example, or to have backup resources ready just in case.

If you plan in advance to handle such problems, you will have more options for dealing with them, which will lessen stress.

"A strategy enables you to fulfill your promises in the best possible way. And the only way to do this is through a system. As most managers have experienced but few have understood, there is simply no way in the world to truly manage anything without one."

—Michael Gerber,
author of *The E-Myth Manager*

STRATEGIC MANAGEMENT

If you are managing many projects on a continuous basis, you are managing a "portfolio" of projects. To do this effectively, you not only have to manage each individual project, you also have to decide how resources and budgets are split between projects in the portfolio.

In managing a project portfolio, you will typically find that resources such as people and materials are shared across many projects. This could require allocating the same resources to different projects at different times. Instead of estimating one project at a time, you should do multiple estimates at once and share data from

Dos & Dont's ☑

HOW TO JUGGLE MANY PROJECTS

When you have many projects going at once, bear these points in mind:

☐ Do take a larger view by looking at projects as interrelated elements in a system.

☐ Do develop a strategy to manage many projects at once.

☐ Do manage how resources and budgets are split between projects.

☐ Do plan on sharing resources across many projects and using the same resources on different projects at different times.

☐ Do estimate multiple projects at the same time to share data from one to the next.

Dos & Dont's ☑

KEEP PROJECTS ON TRACK

The success of your project has every–thing to do with how you manage it.

☐ Don't create expectations that are so aggressive that you and your team will never be able to meet them.

☐ Don't overlook the impact of other projects on your current project, especially if several projects share resources.

☐ Don't overpromise or undermanage.

☐ Do try to be realistic and objective in developing and explaining the plan.

project to project. Similarly, you will need to develop a standard project timeline as a template that you can then apply to multiple projects.

Managing Concurrent Projects

There are any number of project manage-ment methodologies that can help you manage concurrent projects. These methodologies sys-tematize projects so that the process becomes standard and automatic. Their importance lies in the fact that taking a repeatable, managed systematic approach leads to higher quality, and therefore to a better project outcome.

☐ Don't execute a project plan in a vacuum—get input and cooperation from your team and the approval of senior management.

☐ Do invest time in managing team members' relationships.

☐ Do accept uncertainty and change as being inevitable.

☐ Do prepare for change by managing expectations and developing contingency plans.

☐ Do adapt your management style to each project's needs.

Managers at the individual project level need consistent templates, tools, and definitions so that they can repeat their success from one project to another.

Managing Projects Strategically

As you become proficient at project management, you will rise above the day-to-day project milestones and take a broader, more strategic view of the projects for which you have responsibility. A good way to manage strategically is to pay attention to three basic phases: planning, implementation, and monitoring.

Planning. For any project, always have a plan in place that is realistic, well-defined, and structured. Know the outcome you expect, the deadlines you need to meet, and the resources that are available. Make sure that you bring people on board who have the skills you need.

> "Everyone should feel as if his signature is on the finished product."
>
> —Ray Evernham, NASCAR crew chief

Implementation. Executing any project requires the discipline to follow steps in a logical sequence. However, seasoned project managers know that things can, and often do, veer from the anticipated path. That is why it is important to be prepared for change and to be as flexible as possible.

Effective project implementation also requires that you delegate work to your team members. Make sure you are delegating the right work to the right people. Then motivate them to complete the project as a team.

Monitoring. Monitor the progress of each project continuously. Consider other concurrent projects that may compete for resources, including people. Finally, apply your experiences in completing one project to the successful completion of others.

Essential Skill IV
Leadership & Communication

"Management is the efficiency of climbing the ladder of success. Leadership determines whether the ladder is leaning against the right wall."

—Stephen Covey,
author of *The 7 Habits of Highly Effective People*

Being an effective leader is not a right, it is a privilege—a privilege bestowed by those you lead. A leader is not much of a leader without people who are willing to follow.

This is why the first lesson of leadership is this: *Inspire trust.* People want to be able to put their trust in a leader.

People want to follow someone they can believe in, someone who displays character, someone whose vision makes sense to them. In today's corporate environment, people especially want to follow a leader with high moral and ethical standards.

A leader must look deep inside, examine his or her convictions, and validate that they are in keeping with the goals of the organization. Knowing yourself is important if you are to effectively lead others.

• POWER POINTS •

TOP LEADERSHIP TRAITS

The best leaders possess some of these important characteristics:

- Honesty
- Confidence
- Vision
- Intelligence
- Fairness
- Broad-mindedness
- Courage
- Straightforwardness
- Imagination

SOURCE: The Tom Peters Group, www.tompeters.com.

Dos & Dont's ☑

LEADERSHIP BASICS

Your integrity will be apparent in your actions as a leader.

☐ Do know yourself and your own convictions.

☐ Don't assume people will follow you unless they trust you.

☐ Don't tell people something you don't believe yourself.

Paint a Picture

A leader must be able to paint a picture of a goal that people can attain together. Great leaders convey a sense of purpose and envision a promising future so that people feel inspired and excited about getting there. Leadership requires constant communication so that people know where they are heading and why.

THE NATURE OF LEADERSHIP

Perhaps management guru Peter Drucker said it best when he drew the distinction between leading and managing: "Management is doing things right; leadership is doing the right things." Generally, the focus of managers is driven by organizational needs: accomplishing specific goals and objectives, conforming to specifications or requirements, managing projects within budgets and time frames, administering policies and procedures, controlling processes, and managing work groups.

> "It's a self-fulfilling prophecy—if the leader really believes that people can do more, they'll expect more from themselves. People can accomplish unbelievable tasks if their leader expects them to and communicates it by behavior, not just by words or memos."
>
> —Robert Townsend, author of *Reinventing Leadership*

Leaders, on the other hand, set the direction for people in an organization—and for the organization itself. Leaders establish a vision, formulate strategies, take a long view of problems and opportunities, originate ideas, innovate new ways of doing things, and inspire and motivate others.

Outside the Box

WHAT'S YOUR LEADERSHIP STYLE?

Good leaders tend not to rely on a single approach but use a mix of these three basic styles:

- **Authoritarian** – Authoritarian leaders tell people what needs to be done and when, without asking for others' opinions. This style may be appropriate during crisis situations.

- **Participative** – Participative leaders encourage others to help solve problems and make decisions while they retain the ultimate authority.

- **Delegative** – Delegative leaders offer employees a lot of leeway in solving problems and making decisions and are largely hands-off.

What Managers and Leaders Do

There is a legitimate need for both managers and leaders in a business.

Managers execute plans, maintain order, and get things done. They are skilled, competent, and no less important than leaders. Without effective managers, few businesses could operate efficiently. However, managers may resist change, and they may be less capable of guiding and mentoring people.

Dos & Dont's ☑

LEADERSHIP TIPS

Leadership begins with modeling the right behavior.

☐ Do create and communicate a vision that is inspiring.

☐ Do present the long-range view of future problems and opportunities.

☐ Do develop excellent communication skills.

☐ Do stay positive and upbeat.

☐ Don't ignore the fact that people need to be managed as well as led.

☐ Do understand your own beliefs and values before you try to inspire and motivate others.

Leaders are charismatic, motivational, and inspiring. They are skillful at leading people into the future. Without a leader, a business may plod along but never achieve greatness. However, leaders can embrace change to a fault and may be inept at the rigors of implementation.

To be truly successful at managing people, you need skills both as a manager and a leader.

The people you manage will want order, routine, and structure. They will want you to set specific goals and objectives. They will want someone who can guide them as team members to complete multiple projects efficiently. That is the management side.

At the same time these people will look to you to lead, inspire, and motivate them. They will want you to serve as a team leader, the person who communicates goals, guides their progress, and cares for them along the way. That is the leadership side.

Can You Be Both Manager and Leader?

You will probably find that your capabilities lean more towards one than the other. Work on developing complementary skills that grow your strength in both areas.

It is generally more difficult to learn to lead than to learn to manage. While you can acquire leadership skills, some of the requirements of leadership may be deep down inside. Before you

• POWER POINTS •

MANAGERS AND LEADERS

In deciding if you are basically a manager or a leader, ask yourself these questions:

- Where do your capabilities lie?

- What complementary skills do you need to develop?

- What leadership skills do you need to acquire?

can inspire and motivate others, you must have a good grasp of your own beliefs and values. You must be a great communicator. Being a good manager does not automatically qualify you to be a leader. However, if you can demonstrate to people that you can be their leader as well as their manager, you will have loyal employees who will believe in you and follow you.

> "The way to develop the best that is in a man is by appreciation and encouragement."
> —Charles Schwab, founder of Charles Schwab & Co.

PROVIDING FEEDBACK

Great managers and leaders practice *active* listening. Active listening is a way of listening that focuses on the person who is speaking to you and shows that you comprehend what is being said. It can include nonverbal cues, such as nodding and smiling, as well as verbal cues.

Active listeners process what someone else says, rephrase it in their own words, and replay it so that the speaker can validate that the message was understood. It requires some detachment, because your role is to demonstrate understanding, whether or not you agree with what the speaker is saying.

People Want Feedback

By actively listening, you can be in a better position to provide feedback to the people you manage. Positive feedback is, of course, welcomed by employees, but sometimes negative feedback can result in more significant improvements in performance or behavior.

CASE *FILE*

TEACHING LEADERSHIP

In many successful companies, leaders from the CEO on down develop leadership abilities in their subordinates. Former General Electric CEO Jack Welch exemplified this practice. Every two weeks for some 20 years, he spent a day at the company's executive training center with promising managers and executives, listening to them, lecturing, challenging them with hard questions, and in the process demonstrating his approach to quality, productivity, management, and other issues. In all, he reached more than 15,000 employees, transforming the company into what *BusinessWeek* called "a learning organization." During his tenure as CEO, revenues rose from just under $30 billion to more than $90 billion.

SOURCE: "How Jack Welch Runs GE" by John A. Byrne, *BusinessWeek* (June 8, 1998).

• POWER POINTS •

ACTIVE LISTENING IN A NUTSHELL

As a manager, active listening is a vital skill. It has two key components:

- **Verbal and nonverbal cues** – Nodding your head, leaning forward, and saying things like "yes" and "hmm" show that you're listening.

- **Rephrasing** – Repeating what you've just heard in your own words proves you've understood.

Most employees want to know what they could be doing better. They want to receive input that will help them improve. The key, however, is to present negative feedback in a positive way—that is, to offer criticism that is constructive.

People typically take a defensive posture when they feel they are being verbally attacked. Some individuals defend themselves by arguing, others withdraw, and still others may shut down entirely. Negative feedback conveyed in a harsh or angry manner will cause most people to tune out. Unfortunately, if they stop listening, that means they won't hear anything positive that's being said either.

A manager can be demanding and yet offer feedback in a positive way. Try to give your employees examples of what to do right instead of berating them for what they do wrong. Let employees know a behavior is unacceptable, but do it with respect. Empathize with employees and offer them a second chance.

How to Give Feedback

Generally, the best course is to give positive feedback in public and negative feedback in private. Praise is a powerful motivational tool, both for the receiver and onlookers. Giving praise or positive feedback publicly demonstrates that you, as a manager, recognize and acknowledge your employees' efforts.

Negative feedback is best handled one on one. Provide constructive criticism as soon as any

Red Flags ✕◆

TUNING OUT

Negative feedback can be harmful when it isn't presented as constructive criticism. Look for these warning signs when someone is responding to negative feedback:

- Shock and dismay, strong emotion
- Argumentation, dispute
- Withdrawal, nonresponsiveness, silence, apparent inattention
- Nervousness, jitters, fidgeting

Dos & Dont's ☑

DELIVERING NEGATIVE FEEDBACK

Most people want to know how to do a better job at work and truly appreciate feedback. However, the way that you deliver negative feedback has everything to do with how it's received.

☐ Do practice active listening to defuse conflict, avoid misunderstanding, and soften the impact of verbal disagreements.

☐ Don't avoid giving negative feedback if it's warranted.

☐ Don't be overly negative or harsh when discussing performance.

☐ Don't allow yourself to show anger or irritation during the conversation.

unacceptable behavior or problems occur. Ask to see the person for a moment in private. Address the behavior directly and express your concern about it. You should avoid showing irritation or anger. To keep the conversation focused on the desired result—improved behavior—it is best to be straightforward and factual. Taking that tack will help keep the individual from becoming emotional. Allow the person to explain. Make a point of listening actively to the individual's point of

- [ ] Do put a positive spin on negative feedback to make it easier to hear.

- [ ] Don't attack, lest your employee go on the defensive and tune you out.

- [ ] Don't forget that a respectful approach makes the message most effective.

- [ ] Do allow a person to explain and to offer a possible solution to a problem.

- [ ] Do give employees examples of what to do right.

- [ ] Do create a mutually acceptable plan for rectifying a problem.

view. Then, work together in a collaborative way to arrive at a mutually acceptable solution to the problem. Conclude the meeting with an agreement of how and when positive action will occur.

If you handle the conversation correctly, the person is more likely to respect you and take your negative feedback to heart. In the end, your onetime problem employee may become one of your stars.

LEADING DURING CHANGE

It is often said that change is the only constant in business (and in life, for that matter). Change can be disruptive and even demoralizing in a workplace—but it can also allow for positive energy and promise.

A leader has a lot to do with how change is viewed. If he or she is able to cope with change, embrace it, and find a way to lead employees through it, change can strengthen an organization.

> "A corporation is a living organism; it has to continue to shed its skin. Methods have to change. Focus has to change. Values have to change. The sum total of those changes is transformation."
>
> —Andrew Grove, founder of Intel

A leader faces a significant obstacle in leading during change: the status quo. Most people become accustomed to routine. It is comforting to them to repeat the same tasks. They are secure in the fact that they know how to do things and what to expect. They are in control of the situation.

What happens when all that changes? Suddenly, the status quo is turned on its head. Change could mean new rules, new processes, a new boss. Even worse, if change brings layoffs, it can also involve losing friends, colleagues, coworkers.

Leaders Gain Acceptance for Change

The immediate reaction to change is often resistance, even fear. Change represents uncharted

---

LEADERS TAKE THE LONG VIEW

Senior executives who lead change are often way ahead of their people's ability to accept it, according to management consultants William Bridges and Susan Mitchell Bridges.

They call this phenomenon "the marathon effect": leaders who are high in the organization tend to move through the change process very quickly. They see the destination before others even begin the race.

A good leader should always remember that his or her organization needs more time letting go of old ways and transitioning to the new.

SOURCE: "Leading Transition" by William Bridges and Susan Mitchell, *Leader to Leader* (Spring 2000).

THE BOTTOM LINE

territory and a potential loss of control. Strong leaders recognize that this is a common reaction to the prospect of change.

By immediately focusing on accepting the inevitability of change, leaders turn this negative energy into positive energy. They address their

Dos & Dont's ☑

WHEN LEADING CHANGE

In talking about change with employees, anticipate initial resistance. Realize, however, that the way in which you introduce and handle change can have a major impact on employees' response to it. Bear these guidelines in mind:

☐ Do accustom your staff to the idea that change is inevitable.

☐ Do work on creating and communicating a new vision.

☐ Don't try to implement change without a plan that includes both short- and long-term goals.

☐ Do stay positive and enthusiastic to encourage others to adopt a positive attitude toward change.

☐ Do communicate the benefits of the change to your employees.

☐ Don't give the false impression that change will come easily.

employees' apprehension by showing them the tangible benefits that can come from change. They encourage questions and answer them honestly but positively.

Leaders detail a plan for change and ask people for their help in implementing it. They do not give

☐ Do create mid-change milestones to help people feel their efforts are yielding success.

☐ Don't assume everyone will understand the need for change as you do.

☐ Do enlist a group of individuals to be change supporters.

☐ Do work on gaining everyone's acceptance. Negative attitudes can sway even those who support the change.

☐ Do remain honest, open, and compassionate, especially if change may have painful consequences.

☐ Don't forget that change is a continual process that needs to be reinforced over time.

☐ Do assure employees that their efforts matter. They will accept change more easily.

CASE *FILE*

LEADING CHANGE AT HP

After Mark Hurd joined Hewlett Packard as CEO, he carefully studied the organization before restructuring it and cutting 10 percent of the workforce four months later.

More important, Hurd fundamentally changed the massive computer company by streamlining management and reducing HP's business complexity.

Six months later, Hewlett Packard saw a 30 percent increase in profit and a 6 percent increase in revenue, sure signs that Hurd's leadership during change paid had off.

SOURCE: "H-P Net Jumps Amid a Shift in Strategic Focus" by Christopher Lawton, *Wall Street Journal* (May 17, 2006).

the false impression that change will be easy. They convey the sense that it will be a challenge everyone will meet and surmount by working together.

Leaders also know that change is a continual process. In these changing times, change must be the new status quo. The Japanese have a philosophy they call "kaizen"—continual improvement. The understanding that change is necessary to better oneself is one of the reasons the Japanese have achieved such success.

Leaders Change Attitudes

For people to accept change, their attitudes must be flexible, starting at the group level. Coworkers who have a negative attitude may sway those who are positive or at least neutral about change.

Leaders' enthusiasm must be so powerful that it is contagious. Leaders need to make everyone part of the "change team," feeling empowered and in control and believing that their efforts are essential to a successful outcome.

When Change Has Painful Consequences

Sometimes change involves restructuring, downsizing, or other difficult courses of action whose price seems to outweigh any conceivable benefit.

The BIG Picture

GETTING COMFORTABLE WITH RISK

Most change leaders are not averse to risk. Change brings with it organizational bumps, the potential to lose good people, and uncertainty about the future.

However, the rewards associated with change often outweigh the risks. Change leaders create a strong, clear vision, formulate a solid plan, and rally the support of others. They stay focused on long-term success, even if there are temporary setbacks. All these things minimize risk and keep change moving in the right direction.

In the face of such doubt and anxiety, you need to be honest, open, and compassionate. Make everyone feel they are part of the solution, not part of the problem.

In their book, *The Heart of Change,* John Kotter and Dan Cohen detail a multi-step process to help leaders better prepare to lead and manage change. They suggest that you establish a sense

CREATIVE THINKING

Rosabeth Moss Kanter says leaders need to develop "kaleidoscope thinking." They should take fragments of data, construct patterns, and then manipulate the data to create different patterns. This challenges their assumptions about how the pieces of their organization fit together. "Looking through a different lens" spawns new ideas. She recommends getting a fresh perspective and offers the following possibilities:

- Search for new ideas from outside your own industry.

- Work in other parts of your company.

- Broaden brainstorming sessions to include outsiders.

SOURCE: "The Enduring Skills of Change Leaders" by Rosabeth Moss Kanter, *Leader to Leader* (Summer 1999).

THE BOTTOM LINE

of urgency; form a guiding coalition of change supporters; create a vision of the future, communicate it, and empower others to act on it; plan for short-term wins so that people can feel progress; maintain momentum over the long haul; and institutionalize the new approaches to "make change stick."

"How do you know you have won? When the energy is coming the other way and when your people are visibly growing individually and as a group."

—Sir John Harvey-Jones,
British industrialist and business commentator

If you can convince your people of the ultimate benefits of change, you will transform resistance into acceptance. And the goal-setting and teamwork integral to change will help employees stretch themselves and grow—and will energize your company.

Off and Running >>>

You are now ready to put what you have learned from this book into practice. Use this section as a review guide:

CHAPTER 1.
MANAGING 101

- The three "C's"—collaboration, cooperation, and consensus—can help you become a better manager.

- Delegation does not mean abdicating your responsibility. Even when you delegate, it's important to monitor progress on a task.

- Praise should be given in public; criticism must be offered in private.

- A step-by-step plan of action for accomplishing your goal is crucial.

CHAPTER 2.
MANAGING INDIVIDUALS

- A strong business starts with the right staff.

- Training—new-employee orientations, on-the-job development, and formal training—is key to employees' success and motivation.

- Feedback should be given often, not just during annual performance reviews.

- Disciplining an employee is a process that begins with oral and written reprimands and proceeds to probation, when appropriate, and termination as a last resort.

CHAPTER 3.
MANAGING TEAMS

- Teams can accomplish miracles if properly managed.

- Clear steps ensure a team's success: define the team's role and goals, choose its members, foster cooperation, and insist on accountability.

- Match team members' skills to their tasks, formalize their roles, and set the course.

- Motivational exercises, events, and material rewards can all help build enthusiasm.

- A manager provides clear direction, resolves conflicts, and empowers the team to perform on its own.

Off and Running >>>

CHAPTER 4.
MANAGING PROJECTS

- Managing a project consists of seven steps: define the scope, allocate resources, organize your group, build a schedule, do a reality check, monitor your progress, and analyze the outcome.

- Focusing on the project scope helps you assess the resources, money, and time you will need.

- It's important to define precise goals and objectives from the beginning of the project.

- Setting and monitoring project milestones helps keep a project on track.

- There is a relationship between quality, time, and money. Project goals should note the quality that is desired and allocate the appropriate resources.

- Anticipating, assessing, and managing risk is essential.

- Managing multiple projects takes strategic planning.

CHAPTER 5.
LEADERSHIP AND COMMUNICATION

- Leaders inspire trust, share their vision, formulate strategies, anticipate problems and opportunities, innovate, inspire, and motivate.

- Managers execute plans, maintain order, and get things done.

- Active listening, an important skill for both leaders and managers, involves giving nonverbal cues to show that you're listening and rephrasing what has been said to show that you understand.

- Change is inevitable; leaders must help employees accept it and cope with any painful consequences.

- Change can energize a business.

Recommended Reading

The Transparent Leader: How to Build a Great Company Through Straight Talk, Openness, and Accountability
Herb Baum with Tammy Kling
In the wake of numerous corporate scandals, Baum offers business leaders a compelling method to get maximum results by being open and honest in business practices.

Leaders: Strategies for Taking Charge, 2nd ed.
Warren Bennis and Burt Nanus
Leadership guru Warren Bennis and coauthor Burt Nanus reveal the four key principles every manager should know.

Reinventing Leadership: Strategies to Empower the Organization
Warren Bennis and Robert Townsend
Two of America's foremost experts on leadership show how their strategies can lead organizations into a future that includes increased employee satisfaction and continued economic growth.

The Success Principles™: How to Get from Where You Are to Where You Want to Be
Jack Canfield with Janet Switzer
One of the coauthors of the incredibly successful Chicken Soup for the Soul series provides principles and strategies to meet a wide variety of goals.

Good to Great: Why Some Companies Make the Leap . . . and Others Don't
Jim Collins
A best-selling business book, this work distills research on thousands of companies down to eleven that did the right things to become great. The book provides insight into how the heads of these companies motivated people to drive organizational success.

The Daily Drucker: 366 Days of Insight and Motivation for Getting the Right Things Done
Peter F. Drucker with Joseph A. Maciariello
Widely regarded as the greatest management thinker of modern times, Drucker here offers penetrating and practical wisdom with his trademark clarity, vision, and humanity. *The Daily Drucker* provides the inspiration and advice to meet life's many challenges.

The Effective Executive
Peter F. Drucker
Drucker shows how to "get the right things done," demonstrating the distinctive skill of the executive and offering fresh insights into old and seemingly obvious business situations.

The Essential Drucker: The Best of Sixty Years of Peter Drucker's Essential Writings on Management
Peter F. Drucker
This work compiles Drucker's key principles into a single volume.

Innovation and Entrepreneurship
Peter F. Drucker
This is the classic business tome for presenting innovation and entrepreneurship as a purposeful and systematic discipline. This practical book explains what all businesses and institutions have to know, learn, and do in today's market.

Management Challenges for the 21st Century
Peter F. Drucker
Drucker explains how businesses can reinvent themselves to retain relevance in our modern society.

Managing for Results
Peter F. Drucker
Drucker shows how to see beyond conventional outlooks and open up new initiatives that help grow your business and make it more profitable.

The Practice of Management
Peter F. Drucker
The first book to depict management as a distinct function and to recognize managing as a separate responsibility, this classic Drucker work is the fundamental for understanding these ideas.

Corps Business: The 30 Management Principles of the U.S. Marines
David H. Freedman
Freedman examines the organization and culture of the United States Marine Corps and relates how business enterprises could benefit from such Marine values as sacrifice, perseverance, integrity, commitment, and loyalty.

The E-Myth Manager: Why Most Managers Aren't Effective and What to Do About It
Michael E. Gerber
Drawing on lessons learned from working with more than 15,000 small, medium-sized, and very large organizations, Gerber reveals why management doesn't work—and what to do about it.

Harvard Business Review on Managing People
Rob Goffee, et al.
This book provides perspective on the challenges of managing people, from articles originally appearing in *Harvard Business Review*.

Common Sense Business: Starting, Operating, and Growing Your Small Business in Any Economy!
Steve Gottry
This book tells you how to succeed throughout every phase of the small business life cycle—from starting to operating, growing, and even closing down a business. Author Gottry offers practical applications in the real world of small business.

It's Not the Big That Eat the Small . . . It's the Fast That Eat the Slow: How to Use Speed as a Competitive Tool in Business
Jason Jennings and Laurence Haughton
This is an instructive text on how to create strategic planning and creativity to speed your business past the competition.

What Really Works: The 4+2 Formula for Sustained Business Success
William Joyce, Nitin Nohria, and Bruce Roberson
Based on a groundbreaking five-year study, analyzing data on 200 management practices gathered over a 10-year period, *What Really Works* reveals the effectiveness of practices that truly matter.

The Wisdom of Teams: Creating the High Performance Organization
Jon R. Katzenbach and Douglas K. Smith
Authors Katzenbach and Smith reveal the most important element in team success, who excels at team leadership, and why companywide change depends on teams.

The Five Dysfunctions of a Team: A Leadership Fable
Patrick M. Lencioni
Beginning with a real-life scenario, this insightful book reveals how a CEO came to a company and built trust by combating five specific team dysfunctions: absence of trust, fear of conflict, lack of commitment, avoidance of accountability, and inattention to results.

Swim with the Sharks without Being Eaten Alive: Outsell, Outmanage, Outmotivate, and Outnegotiate Your Competition
Harvey B. Mackay
In this straight-from-the-hip handbook, with almost 2 million in print, best-selling author and self-made millionaire Mackay reviews the secrets of his success.

You Can't Win a Fight with Your Boss: & 55 Other Rules for Success
Tom Markert
This guide to surviving the pitfalls of the modern corporate environment presents 56 practical rules that you can use to find corporate success.

Executive Intelligence: What All Great Leaders Have
Justin Menkes
In this thought-provoking volume, Menkes pinpoints the cognitive skills needed to excel in senior management positions.

The Corporate Coach: How to Build a Team of Loyal Customers and Happy Employees
James B. Miller with Paul B. Brown
Founder and CEO of Miller Business Systems, Jim Miller shows how giving customers legendary services and also motivating employees make for a winning combination.

The HP Way: How Bill Hewlett and I Built Our Company
David Packard
David Packard and Bill Hewlett grew their company from its start in a one-car garage to a multibillion-dollar industry. Here is the story of the vision, innovation, and hard work that built an empire.

In Search of Excellence: Lessons from America's Best-Run Companies
Thomas J. Peters and Robert H. Waterman, Jr.
Based on a study of 43 of America's best-run companies from a diverse array of business sectors, *In Search of Excellence* describes eight basic principles of management that made these organizations successful.

Quiet Leadership: Six Steps to Transforming Performance at Work
David Rock
Rock demonstrates how to be a quiet leader, and a master at bringing out the best performance in others, by improving the way people process information.

Mavericks at Work: Why the Most Original Minds in Business Win
William C. Taylor and Polly G. LaBarre
Fast Company cofounder William C. Taylor and Polly LaBarre, a longtime editor at the magazine, profile 32 maverick companies in an effort to examine the "most original minds in business."

*The Cycle of Leadership: How Great Leaders Teach Their
Companies to Win*
Noel M. Tichy
Using examples from real companies, Tichy shows how
managers can begin to transform their own businesses
into teaching organizations and, consequently, better-
performing companies.

*The Leadership Engine: How Winning Companies Build
Leaders at Every Level*
Noel M. Tichy
A framework for developing leaders at all levels of an
organization helps develop the next generation of leaders.
This enables a company to grow from within, which is the
key to excellence, stability, and building team loyalty.

*The Visionary's Handbook: Nine Paradoxes That Will
Shape the Future of Your Business*
Watts Wacker and Jim Taylor with Howard Means
In this book the authors show how nine paradoxes define
the world's business and social climates.

Winning
Jack Welch with Suzy Welch
The core of *Winning* is devoted to the real "stuff" of
work. Packed with personal anecdotes, this book offers
deep insights, original thinking, and solutions to nuts-
and-bolts problems.

Index

Make sure you have all the Best Practices!

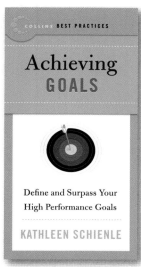

Best Practices: Achieving Goals
ISBN: 978-0-06-114574-2

Best Practices: Communicating Effectively
ISBN: 978-0-06-114568-1

Best Practices: Difficult People
ISBN: 978-0-06-114559-9

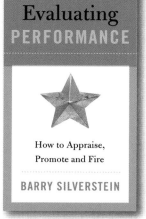

Best Practices: Evaluating Performance
ISBN: 978-0-06-114560-5

Make sure you have all the Best Practices!

Best Practices: Managing People
ISBN: 978-0-06-114556-8

Best Practices: Motivating Employees
ISBN: 978-0-06-114561-2

Best Practices: Time Management
ISBN: 978-0-06-114563-6

Best Practices: Hiring People
ISBN: 978-0-06-114557-5